BEVERLEY

An Archaeological and Architectural Study

PLATE 1. Beverley from the S., the Minster in the foreground. For commentary see p. 87. *Reproduced courtesy Aerofilms Ltd.*

ROYAL COMMISSION ON HISTORICAL MONUMENTS
ENGLAND

SUPPLEMENTARY SERIES: 4

BEVERLEY

An Archaeological and Architectural Study

Keith Miller, John Robinson,
Barbara English and Ivan Hall

LONDON   HER MAJESTY'S STATIONERY OFFICE

First published 1982
ISBN 0 11 701129 0

Published by Her Majesty's Stationery Office for
the Royal Commission on Historical Monuments
(England) in association with the Humberside
Leisure Services Department

CONTENTS

John continued in his see thirty-three years and then ascending to the heavenly kingdom was buried in St. Peter's porch in his own monastery called Inderawood in the year of Our Lord's incarnation 721. For, having by his great age become unable to govern his bishopric, he ordained Wilfrid his priest as bishop of the church of York and retired to the aforesaid monastery and there ended his days in holy conversation.

THE VENERABLE BEDE, *Ecclesiastical History of the English Nation* (731).

The Toune of Beverle is large and welle buildid of Wood. But the fairest Part of it is by North and ther is the Market kept. There was good Cloth making at Beverle: but that is nowe much decayid. The Toune is not waullid: But yet there be these many fair Gates of Brike, North Barre, Newbigyn Bar by West, and Kellegate Barre by West also.

JOHN LELAND, *Itineraries* (1540).

Thence to Beverly . . . which is a very fine town for its size; it's prefferable to any town I saw but Nottingham; there are 3 or 4 large Streetes well pitch'd, bigger than any in Yorke, the other lesser Streetes about the town being equal with them; the Market Cross is large; there are 3 markets, one for Beasts, another for Corne and another for Fish, all large; the town is serv'd with water, by wells walled up round or rather in a Square, above halfe one's length . . . the buildings are new and pretty lofty.

CELIA FIENNES, *The Journeys* (1697).

Beverley is situated 9 miles west of Hull . . . and 180 miles north from London. It is remarkable for its cleanliness, and spacious, dry and airy streets. . . . Its immediate vicinity towards the north and west is elevated and delightfully pleasant, commanding a beautiful view of the town and minster with the rich and fertile plain of Holderness, and altogether may be ranked as one of the most desirable residences in the north of England.

GEORGE POULSON, *Beverlac* (1829).

This is an old-fashioned market town with a 'staid, respectable aspect, as if aware of its claims to consideration'. These claims are founded on its noble Minster. St. Mary's Church is the second object of interest here.

JOHN MURRAY, *Handbook for travellers in Yorkshire* (1882).

v

LIST OF ILLUSTRATIONS

ACKNOWLEDGEMENTS

The authors are indebted to many organisations and individuals who have contributed to this study. For information or advice on archaeological sites Messrs R. Carr, C. J. Dunn, A. Hall, H. Kenward, R. W. Mackay, G. Watkins and R. A. H. Williams; for historical and documentary research Dr R. E. Horrox, Mrs E. Hall and Mr G. P. Brown; for the provision of maps Mr A. Williamson and the Planning Department of Humberside County Council; for editorial work and revision of the text Dr R. M. Butler.

Illustrations. Plate 1 is reproduced by permission of Aerofilms Ltd; Plate 7 by permission of Mr J. R. Chichester-Constable; Plates 2, 3, 10 and 11 by permission of Humberside Leisure Services Department from material in Beverley Local History Library; Plate 4 by permission of Beverley Borough Council from an original in the Beverley Art Gallery collection; Plates 6, 8, 9, 12, and 13 are from photographs by Mr W. Marsden. The front cover illustration is from a colour photograph taken by Mr. P. M. Williams of the Royal Commission staff. Figure 4 is from *The Architectural Review,* vol. 3, by permission of The Architectural Press Ltd; Figure 5 is from a copy provided by Mr D. Neave; Figure 6 is based on an unpublished drawing by Mr R. A. H. Williams; Figures 8 and 9 are based on plans in *The Yorkshire Archaeological Journal*, vols 25 and 34; Figure 10 is from a tracing by Mrs E. Hall, Figure 11 from a sketch in Beverley Local History Library and Figure 12 is based on a map provided by the Planning Department of Beverley Borough Council. Messrs J. Richardson and C. Brown also helped with the maps and figures. Except where stated otherwise, maps are based upon Ordnance Survey maps with the permission of the Controller of Her Majesty's Stationery Office, Crown Copyright Reserved. Map 2 is the result of a survey by Dr and Mrs I. Hall.

FOREWORD

Beverley is one of the many small historic towns which together constitute such a varied and significant element in the English landscape. This study of the town originated in a report compiled by Mr. J. F. Robinson while employed as Inventory Officer by the Yorkshire Archaeological Society under a scheme financed by the Royal Commission and by the County Councils of North Yorkshire and Humberside. It was intended as a complement to his book, *The Archaeology of Malton and Norton*, published by the Society in 1978. Meanwhile Humberside Joint Archaeological Committee, funded by the Department of the Environment and the County Council, was surveying the archaeology of the historic towns of the new county. It was, therefore, agreed that the Committee's field officer, Mr. K. R. Miller, should expand the Beverley report, incorporating new evidence from excavation and documentary research as well as contributions from other scholars. The final editing of the resulting text was undertaken by Dr R. M. Butler of the Royal Commission staff.

In pursuing its national brief, the Commission has recently studied a number of small towns, for example Stamford, Lincolnshire (1977), Dorchester, Blandford Forum and Wareham, Dorset (1952–75), and is currently working in Yorkshire and Humberside. It seemed good sense, therefore, that the Commission should join forces with the County Council in the late stages of the study of Beverley to bring it to publication. We were both delighted at the willingness of Her Majesty's Stationery Office to act as publisher. The Commission is glad as a matter of policy to have the opportunity of co-operating with a local authority. Humberside joins Bedfordshire and Greater Manchester in recent joint publications, while other co-operative projects moving towards publication involve Hampshire, Lincolnshire and West Yorkshire.

GLYN ROBERTS, Director of Leisure Services,
Humberside County Council
PETER FOWLER, Secretary, Royal Commission
on Historical Monuments (England)

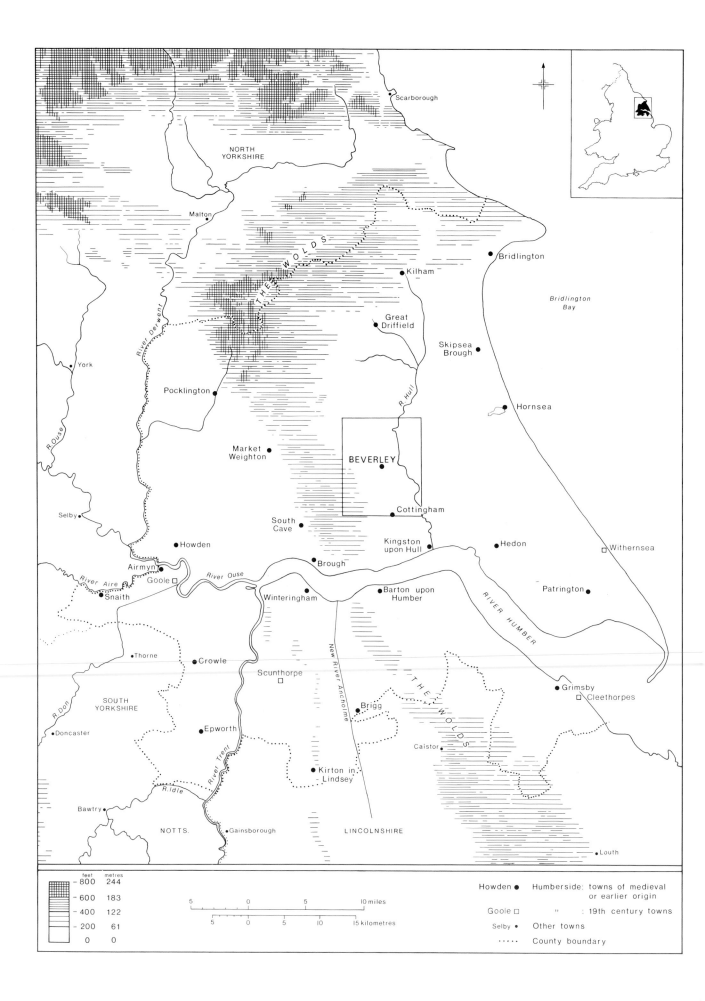

Scarborough

NORTH
YORKSHIRE

Malton

THE WOLDS

Bridlington

Kilham

*Bridlington
Bay*

Great
Driffield

Skipsea
Brough

River Derwent

Hornsea

York

R. Hull

Pocklington

R. Ouse

Market
Weighton

BEVERLEY

Cottingham

South
Cave

Selby

Kingston
upon Hull

Hedon

Howden

☐ Withernsea

Airmyn

River Ouse

Brough

Goole ☐

River Aire

Snaith

Winteringham

Barton upon
Humber

Patrington

RIVER HUMBER

Thorne

Crowle

Scunthorpe
☐

New River Ancholme

*THE
WOLDS*

Grimsby

R. Don

SOUTH
YORKSHIRE

Brigg

☐ Cleethorpes

Doncaster

Epworth

Caistor

River Trent

Kirton in
Lindsey

Bawtry

R. Idle

NOTTS.

Gainsborough

LINCOLNSHIRE

Louth

feet	metres
– 800	244
– 600	183
– 400	122
– 200	61
0	0

5   0   5   10 miles

5   0   5   10   15 kilometres

Howden ● Humberside: towns of medieval
          or earlier origin

Goole ☐   " : 19th century towns

Selby ● Other towns

······ County boundary

HISTORICAL INTRODUCTION

The town of Beverley lies on the edge of the dip-slope of chalk stretching between Flamborough and Hessle, which in pre-glacial times was a cliff forming the E. coast. Beyond the slope to the E. lie the marshlands of the valley of the River Hull (Fig. 1). Beverley was therefore situated on the eastern edge of the land above flood level, and settlement would be likely to appear on this margin. It could, however, have arisen at any one of many places along this edge. The reasons for its occurrence at Beverley and why the settlement there eventually became the chief town of the region are not now clear; geographical factors alone do not seem to have determined its establishment and its later prominence may be due to its connection with the shrine of St. John.

The landscape around Beverley contains evidence of human activity from an early date. Habitation sites, linear boundaries and burial sites survive as surface scatters of occupation material, as earthworks, as crop-marks and as soil-marks visible from the air, or in the shapes of fields and the alignments of tracks and boundaries. A good proportion of sites, by virtue of identified surface finds and evidence from excavation, or by analogy with sites of known date, can be assigned to particular periods (Fig. 3). However, constructions of one age are often overlaid, modified or erased by the work of another and to establish the date of individual features is not always possible. This is especially true of sites known only from the air; some of the recently discovered crop-marks to the S. and W. of Beverley have not been dated with certainty and others represent extensive fragments of historic landscape encompassing several periods. To ascribe these to one particular period would be both premature and misleading; most crop-mark sites and some earthworks are therefore shown separately on Fig. 3.

Many of the archaeological sites in the region belong to the farming communities of the first and second millennia B.C. which have been conventionally divided between the Bronze and Iron Ages. The hill tops around Arras, Newbald, Hunsley and Walkington are studded with round and square barrows. Burials under square-ditched mounds form the main element of the Iron Age 'Arras culture' and their distribution in East Yorkshire roughly corresponds to the area where Ptolemy in the 2nd century A.D. located the tribe of the Parisi.[1] These barrows occur in some number on the Westwood in Beverley, where one of seven near the Black Mill is presumably that in which remains of a cart burial were found in 1875,[2] and at Scorborough to the N. On the E. a large cemetery of square barrows near Swine, known only from crop-marks, shows their extension into Holderness. All this places the site of the later town in the territory dominated in the Iron Age by the Parisi.

Roman presence in the East Riding was mainly to the S. and W. of Beverley. Beside the Humber was the fort and *vicus* at Brough, with roads leading to York, Stamford Bridge and Malton. The nearest Roman road to Beverley may be a suggested route through Bainton, Etton and Bishop Burton towards North Ferriby. This could have provided communications for the buildings, perhaps a villa or villas, recorded near Bishop

Fig. 1. Historic Towns in Humberside, showing the location of Beverley and the area covered by Figs. 2 and 3.

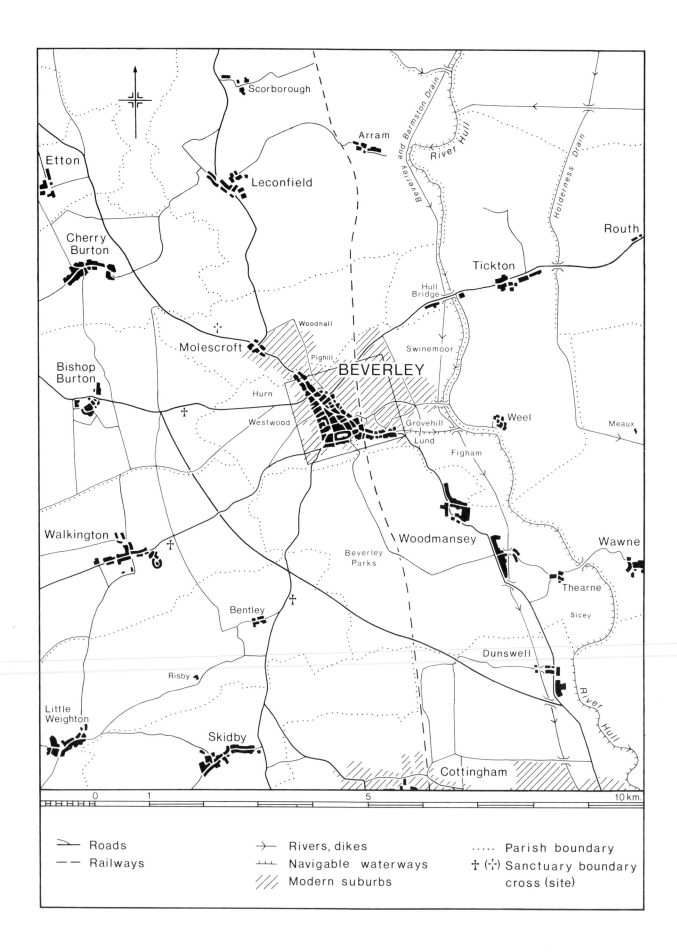

Roads

Railways

Rivers, dikes

Navigable waterways

Modern suburbs

Parish boundary

✝ (⁀̈) Sanctuary boundary
cross (site)

Burton, the kiln site at Woodhouse Farm S. of Lockington, and for other possible Romano-British sites on the Westwood. Roman coins have been found in Beverley at Grovehill, Pighill Lane, Saturday Market Place, and variously in the course of 19th-century drainage work.[3]

The importance of Beverley as a settlement apparently derives from its connection with St. John of Beverley, bishop of York from 705 to 718. Whether or not the monastery where he died and was buried in 721 was actually at Beverley is not definitely established. By the 11th century, however, St. John's connection with the site was widely accepted, and the great church and the community which grew up around his shrine was the *raison d'être* for Beverley's existence until the Reformation. St. John's church was probably destroyed by the Vikings, but according to later legend was refounded and enriched by King Athelstan in 937. The Minster's endowments and buildings were certainly enlarged by the last three Anglo-Saxon archbishops of York and from this time survive the first descriptions of its fabric. The Conqueror issued a charter of privileges and possessions to the Minster, a charter which, although not now extant, was accepted as valid by the Domesday commissioners in 1086. Beverley is only cursorily dealt with in the Domesday Book, being a privileged place free of geld.

From an early date, therefore, Beverley was an ecclesiastical centre of some importance. The archbishops of York, lords of the town, had a manor house beside the Minster from which they administered their widespread liberties over the surrounding lands. The canons possessed several churches, perhaps arising from the Minster's early function as a focus for missionary activities, the right to take corn taxes ('thraves') from the whole of the East Riding, and an extensive and highly privileged sanctuary, comparable to that of Durham. These privileges, and Beverley's importance in the ecclesiastical world, were based on the sanctity of St. John's tomb and not on the church's importance in the hierarchy;[4] the highest ecclesiastical official in the area, the arch-deacon of the East Riding, invariably held the treasurership of York Minster during the 12th century and was rarely resident in Beverley.

Around the church of St. John a trading centre grew up, which was to be of great importance throughout the middle ages. In the early 1120s Henry I granted the archbishop of York and the canons of Beverley the right to extend their fair from two to five days, and in the same decade the archbishop granted to the men of Beverley their first recorded borough charter. At this time the canons had three fairs a year, more than York itself; this and a whole series of later charters show the expansion of Beverley as a trading centre. Beverley cloth, first mentioned in the reign of Henry II (1154–89), was widely sold and highly regarded. The whole process of manufacture was carried on within the town, from the collection of raw wool to the marketing of the finished product, and merchants regularly came there, particularly from London, to buy the cloths. Other trades practised in the town included tanning and the making of bricks and tiles. Beverley also had a special significance as a headquarters of an important guild of minstrels in the North of England. At the Corpus Christi plays of 1390, 38 trades were represented in the town.[5]

The town's commercial prosperity continued to grow throughout the 13th century. Its importance was acknowledged by further privileges and representation in several of Edward I's parliaments (although thereafter attendance lapsed until Elizabeth's reign). From the 14th century, if not before, it was governed by twelve Keepers or Governors, elected annually from the merchant guild and later from a council of 36 burgesses.[6] When the

Fig. 2. Beverley area: settlement and communications, showing the area covered by Maps 1 and 2.

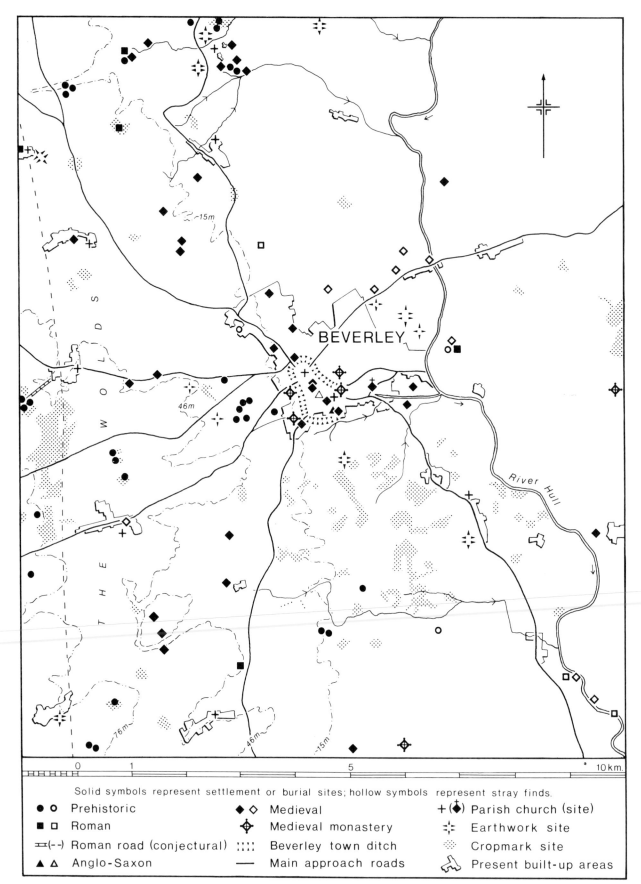

BEVERLEY

River Hull

Solid symbols represent settlement or burial sites; hollow symbols represent stray finds.

● ○ Prehistoric ◆ ◇ Medieval +(◆) Parish church (site)

■ □ Roman ⊕ Medieval monastery ⁑ Earthwork site

⊏⊐(--) Roman road (conjectural) ⫽⫽ Beverley town ditch ⣿ Cropmark site

▲ △ Anglo-Saxon — Main approach roads Present built-up areas

Fig. 3. Beverley area: archaeological sites.

borough was incorporated in 1573 a mayor was added to these and in 1685 the Keepers were designated aldermen. Their accounts survive from 1344.

By 1377 Beverley, with 2663 poll-taxpayers, was the eleventh most populous town in England, twice the size of Hull and about half that of York. From about this date, although the process is not well recorded, it slowly lost ground as a woollen centre to the West Riding towns and, as a port, to Hull. It was still a place of sufficient prestige in 1509 for a printing press to be set up beside the Minster, but that evidently did not prosper. An Act of 1535 refers to 'divers and many houses, messuages, and tenements . . . in great ruin and decay . . . with pits, cellars, and vaults lying open and uncovered . . .'.[7] John Leland, visiting the town in the 1530s, writes of the 'good cloth-making at Beverle, but that is nowe much decayid'.[8] The sudden loss in 1547 of the Minster community, reduced from 77 to two or three, of the friaries, the chantries and the hospitals, wrought further economic damage. By 1599 the town had become 'very poore and greatly depopulated' with 'fower hundred tenements and dwellinge-houses utterly decayed and uninhabited besides soe great a number of poore and needie people altogether unhable so to be ymployed any waie to gett their owne lyvinge'.[9]

When prosperity gradually returned the dilapidation caused by the post-Reformation decline no doubt greatly assisted the redevelopers of the late 17th and early 18th centuries, whose efforts, to Defoe's eyes, had rendered Beverley 'of late much improv'd in its buildings'.[10] Much of the post-medieval building in the town is recorded in the borough archives and, from 1708, in the records of the East Riding Registry of Deeds.

As an administrative centre Beverley has no great claim to antiquity. The Ridings of Yorkshire, although having a continuous geographical history from 1086 to 1974, were only occasionally used for administrative purposes. The East Riding court, of which little is known, met in the 13th and 14th centuries near Kirkburn and not at Beverley. Much local government in the Middle Ages was carried out through a system of county, hundred and wapentake courts, from which Beverley was exempt. It was not until 1889 that the East Riding County Council came into existence and Beverley became the centre of local government that it is today. However, the quarter sessions for the East Riding had long been held there and a register office for the Riding and for Hull was established there in 1708. Since 1974 the former municipal borough has formed part of Beverley District, a division of the new County of Humberside, also including the rural district of Beverley and the urban district of Haltemprice. Many of the administrative offices of the county are in the town.

Notes

1 Stead 1965 and 1969; Ramm 1978.

2 Greenwell 1877, 456; Greenwell 1906, 256. The four possible round barrows on Westwood (TA 02093908, 02093913, 01853960, 02783906) range in diameter from 10 to 15m. and in height from 0.3 to 1m. The square barrows, 7–15m. across, vary in appearance from low mounds to barely raised ditched platforms. They are located at TA 01933903 (group of seven), 01993921 (two), 02033901, 02023897, 02133886 and 01893881. For those at Scorborough see Stead 1975. Other prehistoric finds from Beverley include a Neolithic polished stone axe from the Memorial Gardens, Hengate (TA 031398; Beverley Borough Council Minutes, 1920), a late Bronze Age socketed axe from 'the garden of the Black Friars' (TA 038393; *Sketches*, 27, 61), and another bronze socketed axe from West Close, Molescroft (TA 026408; *Hull Daily Maily*, 15 Jan. 1909).

3 Oliver, 18, 297n.3, 511; Bulmer, 309; Poulson, 16, 807; *BG*, 12 Sept. 1863. In the drainage work and in the deepening of the River Hull hundreds of objects were recovered, including pottery, glass, daggers, spears, leather and coins. Many were in the Stephenson collection, eventually housed in the Albion Street Museum, Hull, destroyed in 1943; a few finds survived without provenance due to the loss of the museum records. See Bulmer, 309; *ERAST* 14 (1907), 61, 64; 20 (1913), 44. Revetting of the banks of the River Hull discovered in 1947 at TA 054397 was thought then to be Roman. Woven withies laid horizontally, about 3 ft. (0.9m.) wide and extending to a depth of 20 ft. (6.1m.) were found in a trench about 50 ft. (15.2m.) wide (information from Mr. D. C. Deans, based on an inspection by the late T. Sheppard of Hull Museum).

4 Although never an episcopal see, Beverley is described, together with Ripon and Whitby, as a 'bishopric' in a survey of *c*. 1100 ('The Shires and Hundreds of England' in *An English Miscellany*, Early English Texts Society 49 (1872), 146). A list of 89 saints' shrines compiled *c*. 1031 includes 'sanctus Iohannes biscop' at 'Beferlic on Hul'; another list in a 12th-century chronicle mentions St. Bertun – perhaps the abbot Brithun – at Beverley (Rollason, D. W., 'Lists of saints' resting-places in Anglo-Saxon England', *Anglo-Saxon England* 7 (1978), 61–93, esp. 62, 71, 87).

5 Champion discusses the varying numbers of guilds recorded, up to 43 in 1467.

6 See Leach 1900 and HMC, 3–4. The Town Keepers changed their title in 1423 to Governors (HMC, 161) but for consistency in references the terms 'Town Keepers' and 'Keepers' Accounts' are used in this report for the medieval period

7 Poulson, 289.

8 Leland I, 47.

9 Poulson, 338.

10 D. Defoe, *A Tour through the Whole Island of Great Britain,* Penguin ed. 1971, 526.

THE MINSTER

Bede refers to a monastery 'called Inderauuda, that is "in the wood of the men of Deira"',
which was founded by John who, in A.D. 721, was buried in St. Peter's chapel (*porticus*)
there.[1] John was the bishop of Hexham and then of York, retiring at the end of his life to
this monastery, which most commentators have placed at Beverley, a name not used by
Bede. The traditional identification of Inderauuda as Beverley occurs in later sources, such
as the 11th-century account of John's life by Folcard, Abbot of Thorney in Cambridge-
shire, a text of the Anglo-Saxon Chronicle which may derive from a Ripon original of *c.*
1050, and a set of notes in Leland's Collectanea taken from an unknown book.[2] Many
such notes and additional stories of the early history of Beverley existed at St. Mary's
Abbey, York, among the Wharton MSS at Lambeth, in the works of Alured of Beverley,
who wrote *c.* 1140, and elsewhere.[3] The traditions they recorded must be read with
reservations. According to Leland's source, John found in Beverley a parish church dedicated to St. John the Evangelist, which he transformed into a monastery and staffed
with monks. He built a new presbytery or choir and constructed to the S. of the old
church an oratory dedicated to St. Martin which later accommodated nuns. The graves
of Brithun and Winwald, two early abbots of this monastery, were later shown to pilgrims
to the Minster. The stone chair by the high altar is by tradition associated with St. John
and may be of Saxon date; a similar chair for a bishop or abbot exists in his other church
at Hexham.[4] On the basis of early monasteries excavated elsewhere, as at Whitby, Mac-
Mahon described the monastery at Beverley as probably little more than a collection of
crudely built oratoria or cells with possibly a refectory, all set in unplanned and somewhat
disorganised fashion around a small monastic church, though Professor Cramp's work at
Jarrow and Monkwearmouth shows that buildings of more regular plan with greater
architectural pretensions could exist in 8th-century Northumbria.[5]

The first element of the place name Beverley is probably 'beaver' and the second is
'stream' or 'lake'.[6] A lake (stream ?) is mentioned in a 12th-century account of miracles of
St. John as surrounding the town and flowing outside the churchyard.[7] The place names
Woodmansey and Sicey to the S. of Beverley, together with the massive peat deposits in
the same area and the marshy land to the E., suggest the watery character of Anglo-Saxon
Beverley. Analysis of the subsoil there should show where settlement was possible when
the land was not drained. However, finds from the pre-Conquest period are sparse,
probably due to the deep stratification, with Saxon levels being buried beneath flood
deposits and later building debris. Pottery sherds found in the peaty layer 2.5–3.5m. below
the surface during recent excavations in Highgate, as well as finds from Lurk Lane S. of
the Minster, probably date from this period. Drainage work in 1891 is said to have yielded
'Saxon and Old English relics'[8] and Meaney lists brooches and skulls from the Beverley
area.[9] It remains to be seen whether the tradition of the founding of Beverley is substan-
tiated by the discovery of an early monastic settlement beneath the Minster or elsewhere
in the town.

The ensuing history of the monastery, as traditionally recorded, includes destruction by
the Danes *c.* 866. King Athelstan (924–39) allegedly visited Beverley after defeating the

Scots and founded a new college of secular canons which presumably superseded the monastic institution. The earliest account of Athelstan's association with Beverley is apparently that given in a collection of St. John's miracles appended to Folcard's narrative;[10] an earlier description in the Durham *Historia Regum* of the king's campaign against the Scots makes no mention of St. John of Beverley. However, Aelred of Rievaulx *c.* 1154 refers to his visit to the saint's shrine and Alfred of Beverley *c.* 1140 says that he ordained that the town of St. John should not only be the head of Sneculfcros Hundred but of all the East Riding.[11] Later medieval sources regarded Athelstan as the founder of the church of Beverley and stressed his bestowal of land and privileges. The anniversary of his death was commemorated annually at Beverley like that of the archbishops. Tradition also ascribes to Athelstan gifts in similar terms at Ripon and Chester-le-Street.[12] No genuine charter from Athelstan to Beverley now exists, nor was any such charter apparently shown to the Domesday commissioners.[13] His position as the 'first King of all England' made him a popular founder figure, but it seems that many of the privileges attributed to him were in fact granted by later monarchs. As in the case of the earlier monastery, it is difficult to assess the degree of truth in the traditions.

During Edward the Confessor's reign the first recorded charter relating to Beverley appears, declaring the Archbishop of York to be its sole lord under the king, and the Minster and the church belonging to it, possibly meaning St. Mary's Church, to be as free as any other minster.[14] The importance of the Confessor's reign in the history of the church is shown in the writs and mandates of 12th-century kings, which in confirming the church's customs refer to Edward and William I but to no earlier ruler. In a confirmatory charter of 1136 Athelstan is mentioned solely as the grantor of sanctuary around the church, whereas the privileges, gifts and liberties are associated with Edward and later kings.[15] Such evidence may put Athelstan's contribution in better perspective.

In the 11th century Beverley Minster was enriched by three Anglo-Saxon archbishops. Aelfric (1023–51) began to build a refectory and dormitory for the canons, caused St. John's relics to be enshrined in gold and silver, ornamented with precious stones, and increased the lands of the Minster. Cynesige (1051–60) continued the building and adornment of the church and built there a high stone tower with two bells. Ealdred (1061–69) completed the refectory and dormitory, enlarged the church by adding a presbytery with a painted ceiling extending to the tower, and placed a pulpitum of bronze and silver at the entrance to the choir, over which was a cross of German work. This pulpitum was probably a combination of reading desk and screen. Ealdred also increased the properties of the Minster, so that it became one of the richest establishments in medieval England, and founded an annual fair.[16] His gifts of lands were confirmed by William I before 1069.[17]

As a result of the punitive 'harrying of the North' by the Normans in 1069–70, much of the East Riding was recorded in the Domesday Book as either waste or much reduced in value; Holderness, for example, appears in 1086 to have been only worth 17 per cent of its pre-Conquest value.[18] Beverley was spared this devastation and, according to Alfred of Beverley, this was a decision of the Conqueror. The Norman army was encamped within 7 miles of the town, so that all the people of the district went there with their valuables. Looting soldiers entered Beverley and moved towards the churchyard; one man with a gold bracelet was pursued by an officer on horseback into the church itself, when St. John struck him down from his horse. After that the king withdrew his troops, confirmed to the church all its liberties and added further possessions.[19]

In 1188 a fire, recorded by Roger of Howden, affected nearly all the town, including the Minster, the E. end of which seems to have been damaged.[20] In 1664 a lead plate was discovered in a vault in the nave with an inscription saying that the church burnt down in September 1188 and that in 1197 there was a search for St. John's remains, which were then discovered and reinterred. This suggests that the fire was a major disaster.[21] In 1213 another disaster struck when the tower fell; its masonry was finished but not the stone spire, and the builders overloaded the marble pillars.[22] The collapse probably caused most destruction in the choir and adjoining parts of the transepts. Little is known of the structure which suffered this double tragedy within the space of some 25 years, but the presence of a re-used capital of Byland Abbey type built into the upper parts of the choir suggests that the first major rebuilding of the Minster after the Conquest is likely to have been Transitional work of the later 12th century. The style of the existing font would support this and further evidence comes from capitals in the interior wall arcade of the W. aisle of the S. transept. These, also possibly re-used in the 13th-century rebuilding, are of a type intermediate between water-leaf and stiff-leaf, and also appear to show signs of considerable weathering.

The Minster remains one of the finest Gothic churches in England, as large and magnificent as a cathedral, and still dominates the modern town. It is cruciform in plan, consisting of an aisled choir of seven bays, an eastern transept of one bay, aisled on the E., a main transept of three bays, aisled to both E. and W., a crossing and the base of a central tower, all built between *c.* 1220 and 1270, an aisled nave of eleven bays built 1308–49, with a N. porch and twin-towered W. front of *c.* 1390–1420 (Plate 1; Fig. 4).[23] A large E. window replaced 13th-century lancets *c.* 1420 and a N.E. chapel was added *c.* 1490. An octagonal central turret of 15th-century appearance was replaced in about 1730 by an ogival dome, removed in 1827. There was an octagonal chapter-house to the N. of the choir, demolished in 1550. Its undercroft was located in 1890–1 by Bilson and Stephenson, who showed it to be of one build with the eastern arm.[24] The attractive staircase and doorway to the chapter-house still survive in the N. choir aisle. The dimensions of the church – 334 ft. (101.9m.) in length, 167 ft. (51m.) across the main transept, 67 ft. (20.4m.) in height to the vault and 162 ft. (49.4m.) for the W. towers – make it about three-quarters the size of York Minster.

An oolitic limestone brownish in colour and of a fairly coarse texture, quarried near North and South Cave, seems to have been the principal stone used in the construction prior to 1213, when the collapse of the central tower prompted the canons to rebuild in Tadcaster magnesian limestone, though re-using a considerable quantity of sound Cave stone for areas of plain walling during the rebuilding programme of *c.* 1220–60. The re-used blocks are of a different colour and texture and, as seen externally, approximate in shape to a square. The nave is almost entirely of creamy-white magnesian limestone. Chalk can also be seen as a walling material. The brick vault over the nave – a construction comparable with the brick vaults of the churches of North Germany – is masked from below by plastering and by the use of stone for conventional vaulting ribs. The bricks average 10 in. by 5 in. by 1½–1¼ in. and are laid in English bond, i.e. with alternating courses of headers and stretchers. Similarly sized and bonded bricks recur at the North Bar and at the Friary.

The 13th-century eastern arm is in 'Early English' style with lancet windows and prominent buttresses on the exterior, bands of blind arcading, and wheel windows in the transept facades. Internally the main arcades are supported on piers composed of a tight cluster of eight alternating shafts. The low triforium has four trefoil-headed arches in each bay with lower blind pointed arches behind them and blank quatrefoils in the intervening space. The taller

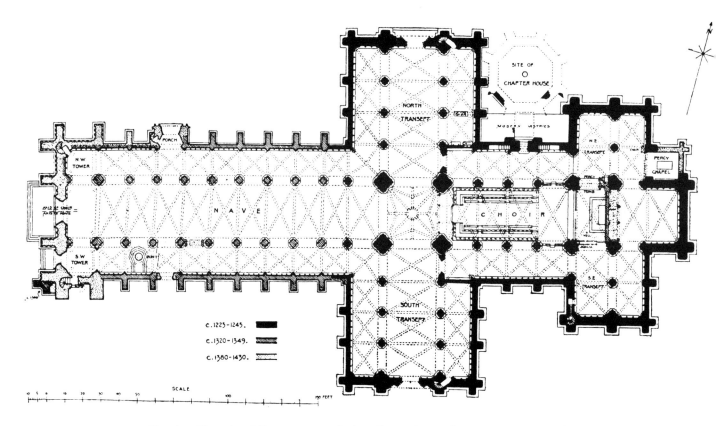

Fig. 4. Beverley Minster: ground plan (from the *Architectural Review*, vol. iii).

clerestory bays have central lancets set in groups of five stepped arches behind a narrow gallery. There is much use of Purbeck marble shafting and dogtooth ornament in both triforium and clerestory. The nave continues the pattern of the choir, though details of the windows and capitals reveal the 14th-century date of this work, which otherwise successfully imitates the earlier build and maintains a uniform appearance, as the 15th-century continuation of Westminster Abbey nave imitates earlier work there. The whole church is vaulted with quadripartite rib vaults. The slim W. towers with heavy buttresses, tall three-light belfry windows, much panelling and niches for numerous statues, provided from 1897 onwards, rise to pinnacled parapets and form a more successful composition than the similar towers at York.

The tomb of St. John is marked by a slab at the E. end of the nave, perhaps at the site whence his relics were translated to a shrine of precious materials made in 1305 by Roger de Farringdon, a London goldsmith. This was set on a splendid stone screen of *c.* 1334 behind the high altar, adjoined on the N. by the 'Percy shrine', an elaborately decorated gabled stone canopy with delicately carved foliage and figures. This sheltered the tomb of either Eleanor de Percy (d. 1328) or Idonea de Percy (d. 1365). To the S. of the altar are wooden sedilia of *c.* 1345 in the style of the Percy shrine. Other outstanding fittings are the 68 choir stalls of *c.* 1520 with their varied misericords, the lead statues by William Collins of Athelstan and St. John from the former choir screen which was replaced by one designed by Gilbert Scott in 1880, the Schnetzler organ of 1767 on the screen, and the late 12th-century font of Frosterley marble with a cover of 1713. The remaining medieval stained glass has been collected in the E. window. Two medieval bells survive: Brithun, cast in Leicester *c.* 1370, and Peter. There is a tread-wheel crane of after 1565 above the crossing for raising building materials, and the oldest parts of the nave roof resemble roofs at Lincoln in design, though parts of the steeply-pitched, lead-covered roofs were renewed in the 18th century.

The loss of most of the Minster's endowments at the dissolution of the college led to a gradual dilapidation of the building, which required restoration from 1716 to the early 1730s, with the employment of some 400 Beverley building craftsmen, their apprentices and labourers. Among the few 'outsiders' were Nicholas Hawksmoor and William Thornton, under whose joint responsibility the work was done, Joseph Burton of York, who repaired the medieval stained glass, Mr. Bagnall, who did the stucco work, and Mr. Pate, the architectural stone carver. The leaning facade of the N. transept was moved back to a vertical position by means of a wooden frame designed by Thornton. Stone from the ruins of St. Mary's Abbey, York, was used in the repairs. The pressure of a growing congregation was met by providing pews and wooden galleries, dismantled in 1826. The Minster was again restored by Gilbert Scott from 1863 to 1880.

St. Martin's Chapel was formerly attached to the S. side of the nave and may have perpetuated the site of a pre-Conquest church.[25] A great cross set at the boundary of St. Martin's altar is mentioned in an account of the miraculous cure of a boy who fell from the Minster roof while watching an Easter play.[26] Originally one of the eight altars within the Minster, St. Martin's was probably removed to this chapel in the first half of the 14th century. It had its own vicar and appears to have served as a kind of parish church during the rebuilding of the Minster. Beneath it lay an undercroft or crypt. Traces of masonry thought to have some connection with this chapel are visible at the base of the S. wall of the S.W. tower and a stone pavement was uncovered in this area in the early 19th century. The chapel is said by MacMahon to have been destroyed in 1550 and is not shown in Daniel King's view of the S. side of the Minster of 1656.[27] Others maintain that the chapel was demolished in the 18th century, when the S. wall arcading and some aisle windows of the Minster were rebuilt in quasi-medieval style where it abutted on the greater church.

The collegiate church, with its nine canons or prebendaries, their vicars-choral, precentor, chancellor, sacrist or treasurer and clerks, was ruled by a provost. The earliest offices seem to be his and the seven prebends of SS. Andrew, James, Martin, Michael, Mary, Peter and Stephen, which may well go back to the 11th century and the time of Archbishop Thomas of Bayeux. The organisation of the prebends may reflect even earlier arrangements.[28] In the 13th century two further prebends were added, those of St. Katherine and St. Leonard, the latter being held by successive archbishops of York.[29] The college was dissolved in 1548, when the Minster became a parish church with one of the vicars-choral as its minister and three assistant curates chosen from the lesser clergy. The sites of buildings associated with the collegiate era lie around the Minster. Leland wrote: 'the Prebendaries Houses stand round aboute St. John's Church Yard. Wherof the Bishop of York hath one motid but al yn Ruine. The fairest Part of the Provostes House is the Gate and the Front'.[30]

The archbishop's house mentioned by Leland lay to the S. of the Minster within the moated enclosure known as *Hall Garth* (TA 03753912).[31] Only the S. and S.E. sides of the moat survive, since the N. side was filled in about 1807 and the W. side late in the 19th century. Excavations for a new sewer in April 1980 revealed the E. abutment of a timber bridge which spanned the moat near its N.W. corner (TA 03693915). The size and arrangement of the timbers suggested that they may have supported lifting gear for a drawbridge, and from the method of construction a late 13th to early 14th-century date seems likely. Exploratory trenches dug across Long Lane, which partly overlies the moat, revealed the remains of the W. abutment.[32] Stones from the house in Hall Garth were removed in 1548 to construct a hunting lodge in Beverley Parks[33] but many traces of buildings are still visible on the platform. The Hall Garth or Admiral Duncan Inn formerly stood within the N.E. corner of the moated area (TA 03753919) and had once housed the court of the provost, or of the Bedern. Poulson and others allude to surviving traces inside the inn of the old court and gaol. The inn also housed the manorial court of Beverley Watertowns, the manor to the S. of Beverley, held by the archbishop until 1545. The building was demolished in 1958 without architectural record and no further details of these remains have been traced.

In 1947 R. Carr and K. A. MacMahon carried out excavations at Hall Garth, largely restricted to uncovering sections of walling to the S. of the inn. These walls, many of which are still visible as low banks, were found to be up to 4 ft. (1.3m.) thick and faced with high-quality ashlar blocks, in places surviving up to three courses high. The foundations of three adjacent buildings were distinguished, of which one, on the S., was thought to contain the Bedern tower of Archbishop George Neville; another building aligned N.–S. may have been a hall.[34]

The Bedern may have been on the same spot, as various commentators have postulated. As at York and Howden, this was probably a close containing the common hall and residences of the vicars-choral; it may also have housed the chantry priests and Clerks of the Barfel or *berefellarii*, probably minor canons. The Bedern Hall is mentioned in 1304,[35] and Archbishop Neville added his tower in the reign of Henry VI.[36] A rental in the early 15th-century Provost's Book locates the Bedern garden in Minster Moorgate and the Bedern itself in Keldgate, a description which could have applied to the Hall Garth at the E. end of the street.[37] However, there appears to have been two Bederns in the later medieval period, since Leland's source alludes to the old Bedern having become the Provost's house, to which the new Bedern, accommodating the vicars, adjoined.[38] Alternative suggestions for the site of the Bedern and Provost's house include St. John Street and the corner of Lurk Lane. Leach believed that the timber-framed hall formerly at the W. end of Flemingate (Plate 2) could have been part of the Bedern complex; alternatively, it could have been part of the residence of the prebendary of St. Andrew, known to have been situated in this area.

Excavations in the area S. of the Minster between Hall Garth and Lurk Lane (TA 03803920) began in October 1979.[39] Work there has revealed two complexes of stone buildings, of which one, probably constructed in the 14th century, replaced an earlier timber hall, and had massive foundations of chalk packed into square pits. A twin-chambered garderobe at the E. end contained remains of wooden bowls and part of a wooden statue. In the 15th century there was a part rebuilding in brick and to the S. a courtyard paved with pitched stones replaced a pond. Stratified archaeological deposits extend to a depth of 1.5m. or more, and boundary ditches, together with residual pre-Conquest pottery, are evidence of Saxon occupation. These buildings are aligned parallel to the Minster but it is too early to say whether, as seems more likely, they represent the former Bedern/Provost's house or a prebendal residence.

The prebendaries' houses. In the Chapter Act Book for 1313–14 the house of the prebendary of St. Martin on the N. of the Minster is described as small and in disrepair, except for the stables and the room over the gate. A new hall, chapel, kitchen, brewhouse, bakery and room by the gate were subsequently built; timber from the old hall was used in the kitchen.[40] In 1376 the prebendary exchanged part of the garden of this house with the archbishop, so that he could extend his garden and the archbishop could have an area 147 ft. by 19 ft. for a plot on which shops could be built.[41] The conversion of prebendal lands for commercial uses was not new, since in 1307 the prebendary of St. Peter granted 'eight shops lately built on my prebend, in length from land of St. Katherine's prebend to that of St. Mary, and in breadth between the high street called Fishmarketgate and the wall situate on my prebend'.[42] These properties evidently lay near Wednesday Market but whether they contained the prebendary's house is not clear.

Prebendal residences are known to have extended around the S. and E. sides of the Minster Yard. In 1319 Henry Carlton, prebendary of St. Stephen, left 'a messuage in Lortegate' next to his prebendal mansion to the vicars of St. John,[43] and nearby, on the S. side of Flemingate, stood the residence of the prebendary of St. Andrew, described in 1318 and 1322 as 'dilapidated', and in 1585 as 'a messuage tenement or mansion house, two little garden places, one dovecot and one close, commonly called St. Andrews Pre-

PLATE 2.   The E. end of the Minster from Flemingate, from a late 19th-century postcard.

bend'.[44] The same grant of 1585 mentions a 'hall garth' in Eastgate 'commonly called St. James prebend garth', also in disrepair in the early 14th century.[45] The poor condition of these houses was presumably due to the fact that many prebendaries were, like those of York and elsewhere, virtually permanent absentees. In the first years of the 13th century, for instance, only three were resident in Beverley.

The chancellor, precentor and sacrist, however, were supposed to be continually resident. The 15th-century Provost's Book locates their houses in Minster Moorgate, that of the chancellor lying in *Ryngandlan* on the N. side of that street. The master of the house of St. Giles and the chaplain of St. Anne's chantry also had houses in Minster Moorgate.[46] The only visible remnant of the whole complex of ecclesiastical houses is 6–11 St. John Street, probably dating from *c.* 1500. When No. 9 was restored in 1974 its front wall was found to rest on a dressed stone wall of considerable depth, 3 ft. thick, from an earlier, possibly 14th-century, building.[47]

In 1973 a rescue excavation was carried out on a site in Minster Moorgate, 60m.–100m. W. of the Minster Yard.[48] The natural subsoil lay at a depth of 1.75m. and cut into it was a V-shaped ditch of uncertain date. At a slightly higher level were found a 'lath floor' and a 'basket-lined trench', perhaps remains of a small 13th-century tanning complex; finds nearby included much leatherwork, mostly footwear. These features lay below peat and clay layers, taken to represent flooding from the River Hull, above which was evidence of 15th-century domestic occupation. By the mid-16th century, perhaps as a consequence of the transfer of ecclesiastical holdings to lay ownership, occupation had ended and the next activity on the site was represented by 19th-century terraced houses. The street frontage was not examined.

The Minster Bow is first mentioned in the Keepers' Accounts for 1407; in the mid-15th century it is listed as the penultimate station on the Corpus Christi and Pater Noster play circuits, and in 1502/3 repairs were carried out on a vault or enclosed sewer there. Town rents in 1494 include payment for a plot of land 'at Mynsterbow' but neither this nor any other reference reveals its position.[49] If it was an arched gateway, an interpretation by no means certain, its name implies some kind of enclosure, but even so it may have served as an entrance to one of the courts near the Minster rather than to a close like that at York. With six medieval streets converging on the Minster Yard more references to this and other close entrances might be expected.

The Minster Grammar School was the responsibility of the chancellor. First attested in the early 12th century,[50] the school probably occupied the same site as its post-Reformation successor, which lay in the S.W. corner of the Minster Yard (TA 03703919). This building, constructed by the Corporation about 1606–10, comprised a schoolroom and a master's house, added to in 1702 and 1736.[51] In 1816 it was demolished and replaced by a new building in Keldgate which was in turn demolished in 1890.

Notes

1 Bede, HE v. 2, 6, ed. Colgrave and Mynors, 456–69.
2 Hearne 1774, IV, 99–104. Leach 1903, 347–53.
3 Alfred (Alured) of Beverley, sacrist of the Minster *c.* 1140 has been confused by some with his contemporary St. Aelred of Rievaulx. His chronicle, based in part on Geoffrey of Monmouth, covers the legendary or real history of Britain from Brutus to 1129 and was edited by Hearne in 1716. Notes on the liberties and antiquity of St. John's church, also by him, appear in Surtees Soc. Pub. 5 (1837). See also Raine 1879, lix, lx.
4 Taylor and Taylor, I, 63; III, 1062.
5 MacMahon 1973, 7. Cf. Cramp, R. in Wilson, 201–52 and Fletcher, E., 'The influence of Merovingian Gaul on Northumbria in the seventh century', *Med. Arch.*, 24 (1980), 69–86.
6 Smith, 193.
7 Raine 1879, 300, 306, 307: 'lacum defluentem extra coemiterium . . lacus circumeuntis villam'.
8 Bulmer, 309.
9 Meaney, 282.
10 Raine, 1879, 263–4.
11 Squire, 92 and n. 64; Surtees Soc. 5 (1837), 101.
12 Farrer, 95, 107–8.
13 Farrer, 94–5.

14 Farrer, 85–6; Cronne, H.A. and Davis, R.H.C. (ed.), *Regesta Regum Anglo-Normannorum III* (Oxford, 1968), no. 99.

15 Farrer, 94.

16 Cooper, 17, 22, 27; Raine 1886, 343–4, 353. 'Veterem quoque ecclesiam adjecto novo presbyterio ampliavit . . . totamque ecclesiam a presbyterio usque ad turrim ab antecessore suo Kinsio constructam, superius opere pictoris, quod caelum vocant, auro multiformiter intermixto, mirabili arte constravit. Supra ostium etiam chori pulpitum opere incomparabili, aere argentoque fabricari fecit, et ex utraque parte pulpiti arcus, et in medio supra pulpitum arcum eminentiorem crucem in summo gestantem, similiter ex aere, auro, et argento, opere Theutonico fabrefactos erexit'.

17 Farrer, 87–8.

18 Brooks, 39.

19 Raine 1879, 266–9.

20 Stubbs, 354.

21 Poulson, 666-7, 680-1.

22 Raine 1879, 345–7; translations of this are given by Harvey, 39–40 and Salzman, 377–8.

23 For architectural accounts see Hiatt 1897; MacMahon 1967; Pevsner 1972, 169–179; Hall and Hall 1973, 7–27, 33; Forster and Brown 1979; Cobb 1980, 52–63. Other sources are Poulson, 513–707; Oliver, 188–90; Sheahan and Whellan, 228–61; Sketches, 21; Sheahan, 86; Nolloth 1952; and MacMahon 1973, 24–9, 39–40, 59–61. The Percy Shrine is discussed in Evans, 171–2 and the treadwheel crane, illustrated by MacMahon 1967, 18 and by Hall and Hall, 12, is studied by Hewett, 70–71.

24 Bilson and Stephenson 1895, 425–32.

25 The Town Minutes for 1425 refer to 'St. Martin's altar in the chapel over the charnel in the Minster Yard' (Leach 1903, 340). Note also the discovery in 1889 of skeletons and other human remains in St. John Street and others around the Minster (BI, 20 April 1889). Oliver (26 n. 43) also refers to sarcophagi found in the Minster Yard, only a few feet below the surface.

26 Raine 1879, 328–9.

27 King, D., *The Cathedrall and Conventual Churches of England and Wales, orthographically delineated*, 1656. See G. Cobb, *Antiquaries Journal*. 54 (1974), 299–301. The view of Beverley is reproduced in Hiatt, 7.

28 For details of the organisation of the college see Leach 1897, xxxiii–lxxvi; *VCH*, 353–9; MacMahon 1973, 22–24. Thompson, 175–8 discusses its constitution which he considered to be 'an instance of the survival of a pre-Conquest chapter, the main character of which was retained in spite of later accretions.' Bilson 1917, 226–31 explains how the 68 existing choir stalls were allocated with the dignitaries below the prebendaries.

29 Poulson, 602–3.

30 Leland I, 46. Extracts from Leland are taken from L.T. Smith's edition of the Itinerary and from Hearne's edition of the Collectanea. For the Beverley entry in the Itinerary see also *YAJ* 10(1889), 246–7 and 470.

31 Poulson, 791–2; Oliver, 275; *Sketches*, 63; Leach 1897, li; Leach 1903, 352; MacMahon 1973, 40; Forster and Brown, 9.

32 Information from Mr. P. Armstrong (Humberside County Council Archaeological Unit) and the late S. E. Rigold (Ancient Monuments Inspectorate). The timbers have been lifted and at the time of writing are in store in a local dyke. Their future is uncertain. Tree-ring analysis suggests that they were felled 1315–30 (*Current Archaeology* 7 (1981), 137–8).

33 PRO Exchequeur Accounts Various E101/458/24.

34 Information from Mr. R. Carr of Hull Road and Mr. L. Parker of St. John Street, Beverley, who have plans and photographs of the excavations. Features shown in Hall Garth on Map 1 are derived from air photographs and from Mr. Carr's sketch plans and are necessarily interim.

35 Leach 1897, 8.

36 Leach 1897, li; Leach 1903, lxxxv.

37 Leach 1903, 316. The Keldgate section mentions 'the Berfellars in the Bedern'.

38 Leach 1903, 345; Hearne IV, 103; Leland I, 46. Leland's account leaves room for speculation, and some (e.g. Forster and Brown, 9) believe that the Provost's house may have been in Hall Garth.

39 Interim accounts are Armstrong, *Med. Arch.* 24 (1980), 252–3, and *Current Archaeology* 7 (1981), 136–8.

40 Leach 1897, 32.

41 Brown 1897, 38.

42 Leach 1897, 206. Note the use of the term '*altam viam de Fishmarket gate*'. Cf. also Brown 1906, 133.

43 Leach 1897, 369. 'A garden wall of St. John in Lortegate' is mentioned in 1307 (Leach 1897, 181) and there is a possible description of the contents of a Beverley prebend in the inventory of Canon William Duffield, who in 1445 had a house in *Lort Lane* (Raine 1864, 137–8).

44 Leach 1897, 353; Leach 1903, 17; Poulson, App. 36.

45 Poulson, App. 36; Leach 1897, 92; Leach 1903, 125.

46 Leach 1903, 317, 321. The location of the chancellor's house on the N. side of Minster Moorgate is based on the assumption that *Ryngandlan* is the same as the *Rygoldlane* which lay between Minster Moorgate and Fishmarketmoorgate in 1435 (HMC, 21).

47 Notes by I. and E. Hall, *Highgate 1977*, for the Beverley Friary Preservation Trust.

48 *YAJ* 47 (1975), 6; *Med. Arch.* 19 (1975), 244; S. R. Harrison and E. J. Carlisle, 'Minster Moorgate, Beverley, 1973' (typescript interim report).

49 See the Town Keepers' Account Rolls (BBR) for those years and HMC, 133, 143. A liturgical play was performed on the N. side of the Minster *c*. 1217–20 (MacMahon 1973, 25 and Raine 1879, 328–9).

50 Poulson, 452; Oliver, 277–80; Bulmer, 351; Leach 1899, xxxix–lvi, 80c–140; Dennett, 191; MacMahon 1958, xv, 115.

51 It is illustrated in Poulson, facing p. 453.

Fig. 5.   William Burrow's map of Beverley, 1747, from a tracing of the original in Beverley Borough Records.   The shading represents built-up areas, but is incomplete on either side of the North Bar.

MEDIEVAL URBAN DEVELOPMENT

At the time of the Norman Conquest Beverley was presumably a small but thriving market town in the shadow of an increasingly powerful church. The growth in the Minster's status and privileges helped the community to become a focal point in the East Riding, and Beverley was spared from devastation by the Norman army in 1069–70. According to Domesday Book:

In Beverley St. John's carucate was always free from the King's geld. The canons have there in the demesne one plough and eighteen villeins and fifteen bordars having six ploughs, and three mills of 13s, and a fishery of 7000 eels. Wood, pasturable, 3 leagues in length and 1½ leagues in breadth. The whole, 4 leagues in length and 2½ leagues in breadth. In the time of King Edward it was worth £24 to the Archbishop, now £14. Then it was worth £20 to the canons; now the same.[1]

In addition to the manor of Beverley there were *berewicks* (outlying portions of the estate) at Skidby and Bishop Burton, as well as widespread lands and churches elsewhere in the East Riding.[2] Disputed lands in Holderness were affirmed by the men of the Riding to belong to St. John of Beverley 'by the gift of King William, which he gave to St. John in the time of Archbishop Ealdred; concerning this, the canons have the seal of King Edward and King William'.[3]

During the Conqueror's reign several charters were issued in support of the Archbishop of York's lordship over Beverley, but not until the 12th century does the town's economic importance begin to be well documented. Archbishop Thurstan's grant of borough status, dated between 1115 and 1128, gave to the men of Beverley the same liberties which the men of York enjoyed and their own 'hanshus' or guild hall as well as economic privileges within the town and throughout Yorkshire, surely a recognition of the town's steady development since the days of the Confessor, if not earlier.[4] Further evidence is afforded by Henry I's grant in 1121–22 of an extension of the Archbishop's fair from two to five days.[5] A later grant to the church of St.John specifies a fair for nine days from Ascension Day.[6] In King John's reign the burgesses of Beverley paid fines in order to buy and sell dyed cloth freely 'as they were accustomed to do in the time of King Henry II',[7] and Spanish merchants, shipwrecked off Norfolk, had cloths distinguished as being from Beverley. The cloth of Beverley is mentioned several times in the late 13th-century Hundred Rolls and letters close of 1319 describe trade with Flanders.[8] Cloth manufacture and wool export were the town's basic economic activities; street names such as Walkergate and Tenter Lane are assumed to indicate where the cloth was processed. The prosperity which this commerce brought promoted the construction of new buildings and an expansion of the town. Although the centre of gravity shifted during the 12th and 13th centuries away from the Minster and towards the market-place, the town was still very much dominated by the church, as represented by the archbishop and by the provost and canons of St.John's.

The 11th-century settlement no doubt lay close to the Minster and along the chief approach roads from York and the Wolds (Map 1). The early medieval canons' markets and fairs were probably held in a large triangular market-place on the N. side of the Minster in the area between Highgate and Eastgate, which was subsequently infilled with buildings.[9] The tenements of the borough's early citizens were probably along the sides of this market-place and along its approaches, spreading outwards as the number of settlers grew. Large-scale development to the S. and W. was inhibited by the low-lying, poorly-drained land, and any initial expansion probably occurred along the highway to the N. and down Flemingate to the S.E., with limited movement to land W. of the Minster taking place from the 13th century onwards.

With the expansion of regional trade and the rapid growth of the cloth industry in the 12th and 13th centuries, commercial interests and trading came to dominate the life of Beverley and it was the market, rather than the Minster, that clearly influenced the later medieval plan. A new market-place comparable in size to the earlier one was laid out alongside the principal thoroughfare, just over 500m. N.W. of the Minster. This site offered much greater scope for expansion than the marshy moorland near the church and, although it was further away from Beckside and the S. approach roads, the other principal routes from York, from the Wolds and from Holderness either converged on this area already or could be diverted towards it by judicious siting of gateways through the town defences. There is some evidence that this happened with the roads from York and from Hessle, which once ran more directly to the Minster. If allowances are made for irregularities caused by watercourses and perhaps by earlier established N.–S. streets, it is possible to see the new market-place, the subsidiary streets, the town ditch and St. Mary's church as components of the same over-all plan, designed to encourage the growth of the borough. The earliest recorded dates for the town ditch and the *Alta Via,* the traditional date for the foundation (or renewal) of St. Mary's, and the age of its earliest surviving masonry, all suggest that the basic pattern was established by the mid 12th century, though the area may only have been developed seriously during the 13th century.

The adoption of St. Mary's church by many trade guilds, especially those associated with the cloth industry, and the substantial enlargements of the building undertaken from the late 12th century onwards, testify to the vigour and prosperity of the town. The increasing emphasis placed on this church by the merchant class and townspeople in general was recognised in 1269 when a vicarage was instituted there, and St. Mary's, though it only became a parish church in the 17th century, subsequently assumed the role of the 'town's' church. Its development, like that of St. Nicholas' church at the Beck, thus characterises the expansion of the medieval borough. Just how closely the town's churches and dependant chapels embody the histories of their respective parishes and neighbourhoods is a question which can only be resolved by a long-term programme of documentary research and excavation.

The presence of several streams running through the site of Beverley ensured that its shape was elongated and that many of its streets were winding. Walkerbeck, for instance, still runs intermittently through the town from Westwood to Long Lane basically along its medieval course. The piecemeal culverting of the stream was completed and reinforced by a sewerage scheme of 1894, which finally put an end to its role as the town's main sewer.[10] A stream which skirted the properties on the N. side of Barley Holme and joined the Beck at Low Bridge was also known as Walkerbeck. Possibly a branch of the Walkergate stream, it may have flowed alongside Hellgarth Lane, but its full course has yet to be established.[11]

The Beck was instrumental in the commercial success of the town. Its canalisation was traditionally ascribed to Archbishop Thurstan, who encouraged the townsfolk 'to make a channel from the river of sufficient depth to carry barges'.[12] The date of this work is unknown, although the existence of St. Nicholas' church close to the head of the waterway by the mid 12th century attests to the early development of a trading community nearby. Later town records give details of various maintenance works undertaken on the Beck and of the Town Keepers' attempts to organise trade and industry in the Beckside area, which was certainly the most active and perhaps the most prosperous of the borough's suburbs (see pp. 30–33).

MARKET-PLACES

Specific market place names appear relatively late: *Fishmarket* in the 13th century, *Souter* or *Shomarket* and *le Cornmarket* in the 14th century, Wednesday Market in the mid 15th century and Saturday Market in 1577. The evocative name *Goodechepelane*, off the *Alta Via*, is first recorded in 1329. The caution with which such market names should be treated is illustrated by the record of a trader fined in 1446 for selling fish in the Wednesday Market 'when time out of mind a fish market has been held in the cornmarket every year from St. Mark's day to Corpus Christi day'.[13] The name Fishmarket was then still being used for Wednesday Market and persisted in property transactions, if not in general use, well into the 18th century. The specialised market kept individual trades together and sometimes, as this incident shows, was reinforced by municipal fiat. In an ordinance of 1364 all cobblers were ordered to confine their stalls to the market assigned to them *(le Shomarket)*.[14]

In the general market-place, the Cornmarket, now Saturday Market, grouping by speciality also occurred. In 1386 there was a fishmarket behind the Dings,[15] and by the 18th century there was a *Smith Hill* (later *Sow Hill)* at the N. end, a *Corn Hill* at the S. end, and a *Crockhill*, a *Butter Market,* a *Flesh Shambles* and a *Fish Shambles* along the W. side of Ladygate.[16] This market-place, which also housed the medieval pillory (on Corn Hill) and the *Bullring* (on the W. side), may originally have extended as far as the E. side of Ladygate and from St. Mary's church to Toll Gavel. The island blocks at the N. end and in the Dings are medieval in origin, but those at the S. end of Ladygate represent later infill. The name Dings comes from a word for 'dunghill' and was earlier *Byscopdinge* or *Bishopdynges,* the hall of the archbishops, which in 1282 was made available to the burgesses for use as a guild hall. This *aula* is first mentioned as early as 1164–70. Butterdings, the modern name for the area E. of the Market Cross, may be a corruption of the early name or refer to a butter market. The name Ladygate first appears

in 1439 and this street was perhaps the early 15th-century *St. Marygate.* The E. side of its S. part is referred to in early 18th-century deeds as 'the east side of Saturday Market',[17] and on Burrow's map of 1747 (Fig. 5) three rows of stalls occupy the site of the later purpose-built Fish Shambles, Butcher and Butter Markets and Corn Exchange. A similar process of market-place colonisation, whereby moveable stalls were eventually replaced by more permanent shops, was no doubt responsible for the adjacent blocks.

Mid 15th-century Keepers' Accounts mention paving repairs 'to the corn market around the Dings and Fischmarket' and give details of numerous repairs to houses and to 'front' and 'back' shops in the Dings.[18] The 15th-century Town Hall at Grimsby and the Toll Booth at Howden both had space for shops and stalls on the ground floor;[19] it seems likely that a similar arrangement existed in the Guildhall at Beverley, at the S. end of the Dings. When the Town Keepers transferred to the hall in 1462 Robert Jackson was paid compensation for surrendering his lease on the shops there, one of which, the back shop behind the Dings, was surmounted by a *campanile* or bell tower.[20]

The history of the S. market-place is more obscure. Although land here was being taken over for shops in the 14th century and Highgate still had shops in the 16th century,[21] the area may already have lost much of its trade to the N. market-place by the mid to late 13th century. The existence of Eastgate in 1239 implies at least some degree of infilling, and the space N. of the Minster was almost certainly occupied by prebendal residences before the end of the 13th century. It also seems unlikely that the Dominican Friary could have occupied such a prominent position alongside an active market, and it may be that this site only became available for the friars as a result of the northward shift in the commercial emphasis and 'balance' of the town during the 13th and 14th centuries. By its occupation of the Eastgate frontage the friary may even have hindered commercial activity and have been partly responsible for the further decline of trading in this area.

The N. remnant of this S. market-place came to be known as *Fishmarket* and its N. approach as *Fishmarketgate*. Details in the deeds to the Minskip messuage in the Crossgarths show that the present Well Lane was known from the 14th century to the 16th as *Fishmarketmoorgate*;[22] before then it may have been *Marketmoregate*. The street's position and name suggest that Fishmarket lay at its E. end (compare Minster Moorgate, 'the road leading to the moor past the Minster'). Further support for the identification of the medieval Fishmarket with the pre-sent Wednesday Market and Butcher Row area comes from 15th-century descriptions of the routes followed by the performers of the Corpus Christi and Pater Noster play cycles. These plays were performed by the guildsmen of Beverley at seven different points or 'stations', starting at North Bar and finishing at the Beck.[23] In a description of the Corpus Christi circuit of 1449 *Fisch-market* is a station on the route between *Crossbridge* and the *Minster Bow*;[24] the most likely position in this section is the Wednesday Market place or one of its approaches. The Pater Noster circuit, described in 1467, was similar, but there *Wedynsday Market*, rather than Fishmarket, was the fourth station, suggesting that the two names referred to the same place or to neighbouring areas.[25] Wednesday Market is frequently identified by 18th-century deeds with Fishmarket Street or Butcher Row, and a will of 1742 mentions 'Fish Shambles' on the E. side of Wednesday Market.[26] This market-place also had a central built-up island. Cottages there were sold in 1719 and 1721,[27] and the block is shown on Hick's map of 1811, the year that it was decided to demolish the surviving property across the N., Butcher Row, end. Weekly trading in the Wednesday Market ceased about 1730.[28]

In addition to these central markets there were other more or less formal trading areas in North Bar Without, Norwood and Beckside (see pp. 29,33). Many of the streets named from occupations no doubt also functioned as markets, and some of the rows and lanes may, like the later shambles, have been part of the larger market-places.

STREETS

The earliest recorded streets in the town comprise the 12th-century *Alto Vico* or *Alta Via* (the 'high' or 'chief' street), *Flammengaria* (Flemingate) and *Newbigginge* (1190). In the 13th century *Forgate, Galdegate, Gilegate* and *Waltheuelane* occur in 1202, *Aldegate* (1236), Eastgate (1239), *Suthbarregate* (c. 1260), *Mynstermoregate* (pre-1270), Keldgate (pre-1279) and *Pottergate*. A revised list of 16th-century and earlier street and place names is given in the Appendix. Some of the early streets are known to have been redeveloped or to have changed their names (see Map 1), but many have yet to be located. An intensive examination of early records will no doubt enable more to be identified.

The *Alta Via* formed Beverley's principal thoroughfare from North Bar to the Minster and as late as the mid 15th century this name was still being used for the Toll Gavel section.[29] The medieval name for Highgate is uncertain. In the 16th century, when the name is first recorded, it was used in the same way as the earlier term *Alta Via* for the 'Highgate within North Barre'. At this time the street running N. from the Minster N. porch, the present Highgate, was known as *Londiners Street*, from the London traders who rented shops there. The name Highgate may not have settled here until the 17th century.[30]

The N.–S. road system was augmented by a series of straight E.–W. cross streets, forming a loose grid dividing the area inside the town ditch into separate blocks or 'quarters'. The blocks flanking the sinuous central section of the main thoroughfare are irregular in outline, but beyond these the pattern, accentuated in places by modern streets, is more distinctly rectilinear. The N.–S. grain of the town is respected by the early cross streets and only one, Well Lane–Champney Road, of which the W. section may be medieval in origin, continues directly into the adjacent longitudinal block. This arrangement could represent separate phases of development, each N.–S. strip or section having been laid out independently. Subsequent encroachments on the frontage at the more popular end of the cross streets have created a funnelling-in towards the high street and market-places, a feature most clearly seen on Dyer, Landress, Well and Wood Lanes.

Beverley's increasing wealth led to improvements such as the paving of streets, well attested in its records from the 14th century onwards, with grants of pavage tolls from 1254/55 (see Appendix). Evidence for the street level having been raised deliberately has come from Highgate, where peat and silt deposits were found like those revealed during excavations at Minster Moorgate and the Dominican Friary; the latter, however, were probably of 13th-century date and likely to coincide with rises in sea level at that time. In about 1890 a drainage trench averaging 7 ft. (2.1m.) in depth was cut along Highgate and observed by W. Stephenson.[31] On a substratum of 'black peaty material' hazel

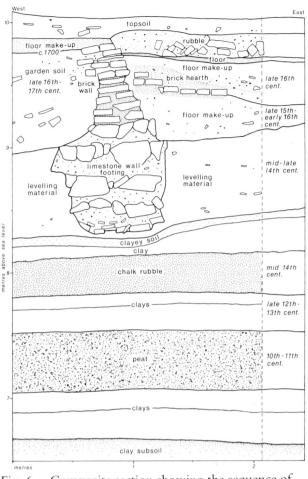

Fig. 6. Composite section showing the sequence of archaeological levels, Highgate, 1977. Dates are approximate.

branches had been laid 'always with their length across the street'. Upon these and in the same direction 'young trees' were laid, supporting a layer of 'large regularly cut blocks' of chalk and stone. Above this foundation the street had been raised to its modern level by a thick layer of soil, clay, stones etc. Stephenson watched similar trenches throughout the town centre and noted everywhere a similar build-up of street level, which he believed to be 14th-century work.

Excavations in the back garden of No.10 Highgate (on the W. side of the street) in 1977 yielded further evidence of medieval reclamation of this area.[32] Immediately above the clay subsoil, 3–4m. below pavement level, were two successive clay layers, each containing evidence of occupation, and then a black peaty deposit up to 50cm. thick (Fig. 6). Sherds from this level have been tentatively identified as possibly 10th-century, and a sample of the organic material gave a radiocarbon date of 1030±70 years.[33] The peat was sealed by compact dark clay, followed by thin bands of dark clay and clayey soil, through which six pits and a post-hole were cut; these levels produced 12th to 13th-century pottery. The next layer was a chalk rubble spread which, from pottery found within it and documentary evidence, can be attributed to the mid to late 14th century. Layers of clay above this and garden soil provided evidence of occupation from the late 14th century to the 19th century. The peat layer represented the deliberate dumping of organic refuse 'from within or around buildings . . at fairly regular intervals . . over a long period', giving an impression of 'an area of open land covered by moist rotting matter'.[34] The peat observed by Stephenson probably formed part of this same deposit. Further sampling and analysis of material from selected sites should enable the age and extent of natural flood deposits and of reclamation or dumping to be determined with greater certainty.[35]

TENEMENTS.

Recent research in other major medieval towns has shown that tenement boundaries can persist for many centuries. Property boundaries in Blackfriargate, Hull, for instance, have been found to remain unchanged from the 14th to the 18th century,[36] and in older-established cities, such as Norwich and York, for even longer. There is good reason to believe that at Beverley too the streets and property boundaries of the central area preserve the medieval pattern in modified form, if not in every detail. The series of strip plots arranged on either side of the main streets and market-places originate in medieval burgages, the urban plots held by the burgesses in return for a fixed rent. The right of free burgage, granted by Thurstan and confirmed by Henry I *c.* 1130, meant that these plots could be freely transferred, bought and sold. This was an important privilege for, when coupled with grants of free toll and recognition of the borough's merchant guild, it encouraged economic and urban growth.[37]

Burgages normally took the form of long, narrow plots laid out roughly at right angles to a main street and parallel to each other, each typically containing a house or shop fronting on the street, with behind it a yard and often a garden. Access to the rear yards was provided by back lanes or by alleyways from the street, many of which would have passed through an arch beneath the 'frontstead'. The burgage arrangement, whereby valuable frontage space was shared out, is accommodated most effectively in a rectangular grid system. At Beverley the combined street and burgage layout is seen at its most formal in the series of blocks on the E. side of Saturday Market, between Eastgate and Highgate, and along the straighter sections of the main streets where there was sufficient space to set out a rectangular framework, as along North Bar Within, Flemingate, and the W. side of Wednesday Market and Highgate.

Elsewhere the plots were adapted to the irregular street pattern, and while in most places the typical 'herringbone' pattern and regular street frontage divisions were maintained, considerable variation in plot length often resulted. Between Saturday Market/Toll Gavel and Lairgate, for instance, plot length increases from 20m. or less in the N. near Old Waste to over 85m. near Landress Lane. Natural site conditions sometimes produced local variations in the plot pattern, as in the Cross Garths opposite the junction of Walkergate and Toll Gavel where the course of the Walkerbeck marks a distinct change in plot alignment. Pre-existing features also influenced the new layout, and the reversed-S shape of the lanes and plots on the

W. side of North Bar Within suggests that they were laid out on the strips of open fields. The twisting or curved profile shared by the plots further S. may also represent former field divisions, though in many cases, as between Saturday Market and Lairgate, the changes in alignment can more reasonably be attributed to the practice of building square-on to a curving street frontage. The reasons for other local distortions in plot shape and size are not so clear; a particularly intriguing arrangement is seen in the Cross Keys – Burgess Yard area, on the E. side of the junction of North Bar Within and Lairgate.

Nothing is known about the original size of Beverley's burgages or how plot size and shape were related to various parts of the town at different dates. Evidence of the subsequent amalgamation and subdivision of plots can often be obtained from documents and from the buildings themselves, at least for the later post-medieval and modern period, but for the crucial early centuries of the town's development the evidence lies below ground and has yet to be investigated. None of the surviving timber-framed buildings in Beverley appears to date from before 1400. All are built with their long sides along the street except for No. 11 Ladygate, which has a jettied gable end (now obscured by later brickwork) facing the street. Examination of early buildings in Saturday Market and Wednesday Market suggests a late medieval plot width based on units of 9½ ft. and 11½ ft.[38]

The physical constraints imposed by the high density of buildings along the main street frontages and the commercial pressures which demand full use of available space have tended to maintain the medieval property pattern in the town centre. In some places long-term institutional ownership, especially by the Church, has preserved early buildings and property boundaries. The areas away from the main trading streets do not display such strong continuity, and the medieval land-use of large parts of the town within the defences is far from certain. Enclosed plots of pasture, orchards and gardens were common in the W. part in the mid 18th and early 19th centuries, and contemporary maps show that outside the main trading areas plots were larger and less regular. However, such recent surveys cannot be regarded as a reliable guide to the character of medieval settlement in these 'backland' areas. In the intervening period the town had not only suffered the upheaval of the Reformation and serious late medieval decay, but, during its subsequent regeneration, property holdings had been consolidated into larger units and land had been cleared for large houses and gardens. This process, already under way by the late 1660s, gained momentum during the 18th century and affected those areas outside the commercial centre.

The history of individual sites can sometimes be traced back from later and better documented periods. Research on the grounds of St. Mary's Manor within the N.E. angle of the town ditch and on the Guildhall site behind the Toll Gavel frontage plots shows that there at least the later medieval plot layout was more diverse and the density of building far less than on the main streets.[39] For the earlier history of these sites, and for the medieval period as a whole in the poorly documented sites on the E. and W. sides of the town, archaeology will be the chief source of information.

Map 2 and Figure 7 provide a good indication of the expansion of the built-up area during the post-medieval and modern periods.[40] Modern streets in the town centre include the early 19th-century Cross Street, Railway Street (late 1840s), Lord Roberts Road (1909), Sow Hill Road (late 1960s) and the conversion of Manor Road into a dual carriageway in 1971. Large-scale redevelopment on the E. and W. sides of the town, much of it within or directly outside the medieval borough, has taken place since the early 19th century. Of two new roads, arguably the most radical departures so far from the essentially medieval street pattern of the central area, work on the Walkergate Relief Road has been completed and that on the link road between Grovehill Road and Chantry Lane is under review.

1747 (Burrow)

1811 (Hick)

1892 (OS)

1950 (OS)

1974 (OS)

0   500   1000 m.

Fig. 7.   The growth of Beverley, 1747–1974.

OCCUPATIONAL PLACE-NAMES AND MEDIEVAL TRADES

The earliest recorded Beverley street name with an occupational association is the 12th-century *Flammengaria (vicum Flandrensium* in 1318), now Flemingate, which took its name from Flemish settlers, probably traders or cloth workers.[41] Flemish cities had obtained their first privileges in England in the late 11th century and merchants from Flanders are known to have been present in this country by the early 12th century. *Pottergate,* first recorded in the 13th century, reappears in the 15th-century Provost's Book as a road in *Grovall* (Grovehill) and may be the 'layn next groval called potterlane' mentioned in the Keepers' Accounts for 1519/20. A *Poterscarth Lane* is mentioned in 1329, a gutter 'beside Potterlane *in latere torrentis'* ('at the side of the torrent', i.e. the Walkerbeck or the Beck) in 1407, and *Potterstartlane* in 1409. All seem to have been in the area between Flemingate and Grovehill, but whether any were the *Potter Lane* shown on Burrow's map is doubtful, for in the 15th-century Keepers' Accounts this street seems to have been regarded as part of Trinity Lane.[42] *Potter Hill,* at the E. end of Flemingate, is first recorded in a grant of 1585. Potters did not only work with clay: the term also denoted metal-workers.

The 14th-century Walkergate and Walkerbeck take their names from the walkers or fullers, who soaked the newly woven cloth in a fulling agent and beat and trampled it in troughs until it had shrunk and thickened. A royal confirmation of gifts to St. Mary's in 1329 mentions 'land in the street of the fullers'[43] and a lane near Walkergate called *Tentur Lane,* a reference to the area where, after fulling, the wet cloth was stretched out to dry on frames or 'tenters'. The lane has not been positively identified but may be the *Tentoure Lane* recorded in the 16th century; a *Tenter Lane* was also mentioned in a sale of 1870 as part of Home Church Lane.[44] Four other references to tenter grounds have been found in later records: in 1578/79 Robert Barbour, clothmaker, rented 'one Tenter Roome upon Norwood Hill';[45] a *Tenter Garth* in the Cross Garths is recorded in the 16th century,[46] another on the S. side of the 'old Hospitall' in Lairgate (see p. 53) in 1697, and a *Tenter Close* of 6 acres 'in Beverley' was sold in 1739 and re-sold two years later.[47]

Couper Lane (coopers: makers of wooden casks) is first recorded in a deed of 1391 which places it on the W. side of North Bar Within, opposite St. Mary's church. *Ferourlane* (ferrour: farrier or blacksmith), also recorded in 1391, lay on the E. side of Eastgate. *Smetheraw* is mentioned in 1392 and *smith's row* in 1450/51; the smiths of the post-medieval *Smith Hill* at the N.

end of Saturday Market were probably whitesmiths.[48]

Fifteenth-century occupational street-names include *Hayrerlane* or *Hairelane* (perhaps from hairers or workers in horsehair) on the E. side of Fishmarket/Eastgate, *Mercer Row* (mercer: dealer in fine fabrics, silks etc.), *Sevierlane* (sevier: sieve-maker) 'stretching from Flemingate to Helgarth', *Bakhouse Lane* (from bakehouse – a bakery, or barkhouse – a tannery), *Coyner* (coiner) *Lane, Pudding Lane* (perhaps from dealers in offal, sausage etc), *Bocherrow* or *butcher row,* probably at the N. end of Saturday Maket place and not the present Butcher Row, *Brederawe* or *Bread Row,* and *Skepper Lane* (skepper: basket maker) on the S. side of Flemingate, near Lurk Lane. *Spyneslane* (from spinners of wool or yarn?), included in a list of paving costs for Walkergate of 1433/34 and mentioned again in 1556, is probably the same as *Spynyshlane,* repaired in 1502/03. *Briddal Myddyng,* first recorded in 1433/34, appears in a variety of forms, eventually emerging in the mid-18th century as *Burdet Midden* or *Lane,* now Dog and Duck Lane. The first element may be derived from 'bridle-maker'; 'midden', like the nearby *Dings,* is of Scandinavian origin and refers to a dung or rubbish heap.

From the 16th century come *Buge Row* (from makers of budge, lambskin with the wool dressed outwards), *Spurier Lane* (spurrier: spur maker), and *Shoemaker Lane,* on the E. side of Ladgate and possibly the same as the 14th-century *Shomarket.* Lorimers Row (lorimer: a bit or spur maker), formerly near the Rose and Crown Inn outside the North Bar,[49] and *Blucher* (bleacher?) *Lane,* adjacent to Beckside, are apparently post-medieval names. Dyer Lane is an 18th-century name for a street known earlier as *Bowbriglane,* from the bridge over the Walkerbeck at its E. end.[50] However, as fulling, tenting and dyeing were probably carried out close together, and as both fullers and dyers depended on plentiful supplies of water, dyers may well have been active in this general area, if not in this street, in the middle ages. In 1429 a *wadiator* (perhaps a dyer with woad) is mentioned in connection with a tenement on the E. side of the 'highway near the Cuckstolepytt',[51] and in 1436 John Dameson, 'littester (dyer) next to the Cuckstolepit' was fined for throwing offal into the Walkerbeck.[52] This Cuckstool (duckingstool) pit was probably in or near the Walkerbeck on the E. side of the town. There was another near North Bar.

Occupations were the basis of many surnames and it is quite possible that some of the streets mentioned above took their names from prominent occupants. Landress Lane, for example, surely got its name from Roger Laundese, who in the 16th century had an acre close 'by a lane on the west side of Toll Gavel'.[53]

The uncertainty surrounding the origin of the occupational street-names, their range of dates, and the fact that few have been located, mean that little can yet be said about the distribution of medieval trades. Place-names associated with cloth making, for instance, come from widely separated dates (only Flemingate, Tenter Lane and Walkergate coming from the period when the cloth trade was at its height in the town) and there is insufficient evidence to point to specific centres of production, apart from the area around Walkergate. However, what does emerge is a general emphasis on the E. side of the town, especially in manufacturing, with even a suggestion of specific industrial zones in the later middle ages (see p. 32). Further documentary research, particularly on the medieval guild ordinances and Town Keepers' Accounts, could add much to our understanding of Beverley's industries in the later medieval period.

Notes

1 DB, folio 304.
2 DB, folios 304, 374.
3 DB, folio 374.
4 Farrer, 90ff.
5 Farrer, 89–90.
6 Farrer, 103.
7 Stenton, 65.
8 Lister, xvi.
9 Allison, 229. The late development of Highgate may also be reflected in the building of the early 15th-century N. porch of the Minster facing down the street; the older N. transept door would have faced directly onto the market place. See also notes by I. and E. Hall, *Highgate 1977,* for Beverley Friary Preservation Trust.

10 Borough of Beverley, *Report of the Borough Surveyor as to the Walker Beck,* 1893, in Beverley Local History Library.
11 BBR Town Keepers' Account Roll for 1494 records rent paid by Robert Rawlyn and William Awmyller for 'the common watercourse of the common sewer of Walkerbeck up to the bridge called parson brygg'. Eighteenth-century references include HCRO Registry of Deeds, I 126/278, I 127/279.
12 British Museum, Lansdowne MSS B.896, quoted by Witty in *BG,* 25 Jan. 1930.
13 HMC, 131.
14 HMC, 71, 72.
15 BBR Town Keepers' Account Roll 1386.

16 HCRO Registry of Deeds x 250/571; u 441/836.

17 HCRO Registry of Deeds a 22/32.

18 BBR Town Keepers' Account Roll 1450/51.

19 Gillett, 2. Work above the shops in the Howden Toll Booth is mentioned in 1547 *(The Paper Book of Ralph Dalton,* Hull University Library Archives Dept., MS DDJ/10/110).

20 HMC, 112, 114, 123, 141, 167.

21 See pp. 12–14. Two shops *(seldis)* in the fishmarket are mentioned in the 13th century (Hebditch, 11).

22 BBR Schedule III/13.

23 MacMahon 1973, 15–16.

24 The Corpus Christi circuit in 1449 had stations 'ad Barras Boriales, juxta Bulryng; inter Johannem Skipwith et Robertum Couke in Alta Via; apud Crosse bryg; apud Fischmarket; apud Mynstir bowe ad Torrentem' (HMC, 133).

25 The Pater Noster circuit of 1467 ran 'ad Barros Boriales, Bulryng, ad ostium Ricardi Conton in Via Alta, Crossebrug, Wedynsday Market, Mynsterbowe et Bekside' (HMC, 143).

26 HCRO Registry of Deeds Q 64/126; M 390/616; Q 388/994.

27 HCRO Registry of Deeds 6 241/543; H 19/38; H 20/39.

28 MacMahon 1973, 56–7.

29 See notes 24, 25 and p. 23, n. 39.

30 Poulson, App. 32; English and Neave, 3, 4; Witty, *BG,* 8 March 1930. Dennett, x, 88, 156–7; Leach 1903, 360. (Smith's identification of Londiners Street with Landress Lane (Smith, 195) is mistaken.)

31 Stephenson, 273–4.

32 The excavations were directed by R. A. H. Williams on behalf of the Inspectorate of Ancient Monuments and the Humberside Joint Archaeological Committee. Mr. Williams kindly permitted the study of his original records. 'An Excavation at Highgate, Beverley, 1977' is a duplicated typescript of 1978 by him. The authors wish to stress that they alone are responsible for the interpretation of the material presented in this report.

33 HAR -2736. 27.8.78.

34 Hall, A. R. and Kenward, H. K., 'Biological Remains from Highgate, Beverley', duplicated typescript, 1978.

35 A layer of peat and of timbers laid side by side was also revealed in excavations at Lurk Lane in June 1980.

36 Ayres, B., *Excavations at Blackfriargate 1977,* Hull Old Town Reports Series No. 7. 1981. The original frontage measurements of the burgages there remained constant, although the plots were subsequently subdivided and there were post-medieval changes at the backs.

37 Douglas and Greenaway, 962–3. This grant contains the first recorded use of the term 'burgage' (Reynolds, 98–9).

38 A grant of 1440 mentions a plot '9 feet of a man's foot wide' and '31 rods long' in *Hayrerlane* (Hebditch, 24).

39 Documentary research was undertaken by Dr. R. Horrox for the Humberside Joint Archaeological Committee. See also 'Development in Beverley: the archaeological implications', duplicated typescript, 1980.

40 See also de Boer.

41 For sources of the other place-names in this section see Appendix, Smith, and the Town Keepers' Account Rolls for the years quoted.

42 Witty suggests that Pottergate was 'a lost lane from somewhere near Faggot Houses on Beckside to Daisy Cottage in Holme Church Lane' at 'the Swinemoor Lane end of Holme Church Lane' *(BG, 26 Oct 1929).* See also the section below on potters in the Grovehill-Beckside area, p. 32.

43 *CPR 1327–30,* 409.

44 Witty, *BG,* 4 Jan. 1930.

45 Dennett, 27. A grant of 1585 refers to a close in Norwood 'late occupied by Thomas Smyth, fuller' (Poulson, App. 42).

46 BBR Schedule III/2.

47 HCRO Registry of Deeds P 310/798; R 2/2; R 2/3.

48 A whitesmith occupied 'a house called a fee farm tenement' at Sow Hill in 1755 (HCRO Registry of Deeds x 250/571). See also Witty, *BG,* 5 April 1930.

49 Witty, *BG,* 14 June 1930, giving no date for the name.

50 HCRO Registry of Deeds R 417/1031; R 435/1072; Burrow's map of 1747.

51 Hebditch, 23.

52 HMC, 111, 116.

53 English and Neave, 3. In 1585 Roger Laundese occupied a close in Lairgate and a Thomas Laundische possessed a close on the E. side of the 'the Kings street' (Poulson, App. 42, 27).

SUBURBS AND COMMONS

The term 'suburb' is open to various interpretations but is here used for areas outside the town ditch or, on the S. and E. sides of the town where the defensive circuit is not clearly defined, for settlement of similar character on the fringes of the built-up area.[1] Maps and documents rarely provide sufficient information to reconstruct the early suburban topography, for not only did settlement and land use in the suburbs tend to be more fluid and irregular than in the town centre, but their inhabitants were also on average poorer and therefore less likely to figure in early records.[2] Suburbs are a barometer of a town's fortunes, and those around Beverley were probably among the first areas to register the effects of its decline in the later middle ages. It is quite likely that suburban development was at its greatest extent in the 13th and 14th centuries and that by the time of the earliest town maps substantial parts of Beverley's medieval suburbs had merged back into the open countryside.

The earliest suburbs probably clustered outside the town bars, around the Beck and along the principal approaches. North Bar Without, Norwood, part of Keldgate, and Beckside formed separate *constabularia*, bailiwicks or wards of the medieval borough. In medieval taxation lists the last three are distinguished as part of the Provost's fee, i.e. under the jurisdiction of the provost and chapter of the collegiate church, and are sometimes listed separately from the central wards of North Bar Within, Walkergate, Cornmarket, *Alta Via*, Lairgate, Fishmarket, Keldgate, Flemingate and Barleyholme.[3] In the case of North Bar Without, Norwood and perhaps Beckside, these administrative divisions coincide with the respective suburban areas, but at Keldgate the position was more complicated. A rental in the 15th-century Provost's Book[4] shows that his fee at Keldgate included properties both there and in the streets to the N., and it is posible that some of the outlying holdings on the E. side of the town were included in the tax figures for Beckside and Norwood. Fifteenth-century subscriptions for men at arms, usually archers, were also organised by ward or constabulary, and in many cases the lists of payments give details of individual contributions.[5] These records together provide a useful indication of the relative levels of population and prosperity in different parts of late medieval Beverley and are well worth further study.

NORTHERN SUBURBS

Evidence for development along *North Bar Without* and Norwood is provided by medieval church properties and town rentals. In 1450/51 a tenement outside North Bar was rented by the town from the archbishop and in the same year William Northorp paid rent to the Town Keepers for 'a cottage built on the common lane near his messuage outside North Bar'.[6] Other cottages and tenements here are mentioned in the 15th and 16th centuries, and when a croft belonging to St. John's gild was leased in 1438 the Keepers stipulated that they were to have free access to 'les gravel pitts' to bake clay (*argillo*).[7] The land adjacent to the E. side of the bar was occupied by St. Mary's Hospital, which had a garden on its E. side, and on the N. side of the York road, just outside the bar, lay Lorimers' Row. Like similar institutions at Grimsby, Stamford and elsewhere, the leper houses outside North Bar and Keldgate Bar were probably situated away from the main built-up area. On the borough boundary about

580m. N. of North Bar stood the gallows in *Gallows* or *Galley Lane* (approx. TA 025402).[8] For that slightly more domestic instrument of correction, the cucking (or ducking) stool, the town ditch was evidently utilised. The *Kutstulpyt* is first mentioned in 1379 and a 'lane called Cuckstolpit' appears in an Elizabethan grant. In the 15th and 16th centuries the cuckstoolpit apparently lay on the E. side of the town, in or near the Walkerbeck.[9] The 'Bar Dike' pond outside the North Bar may have been another, or perhaps a later, site. Yet another position is suggested by Woods' survey of 1828, where the present Tiger Lane, which originally would have extended from North Bar Within to the town ditch, is shown as *Cuckstool Lane*.[10]

The rental of the Beverley Provostry in the Provost's Book lists a number of Norwood properties, most of them tenements and closes.[11] *Stanelayplace, Stapylappylgarth* and *alba via* are among the places named. The latter is presumably the *White Place* mentioned in 1557, and Witty records that 'the house now part of the High School was once Stanley Place' (Norwood House, TA 03303994). The Keepers' Accounts for 1407 mention the repair of the causeway and part of the bridge at Hull Bridge and of the road towards *Northwode,* and in 1435 there is a reference to what may have been a roadside cross at Norwood.[12]

The wide medieval streets of Norwood and North Bar Without probably served as marshalling grounds for those waiting to enter the town, especially on market and fair days, and both areas could have served as market-places for animals or bulky goods, such as hay. North Bar Without is sometimes called *Horsefair* in early 18th-century property transactions,[13] and a cattle market held at Norwood until 1865 may have had its origin in a fair held there under the archbishop's jurisdiction.[14] From the 17th century onwards North Bar Without and, to a lesser extent, Norwood, were adopted by the wealthier citizens of Beverley; by the late 18th century, when the ornamental New Walk was laid out, North Bar Without was flanked by substantial houses.

WESTERN SUBURBS

In sharp contrast to the N. approaches, the areas outside Newbegin and Keldgate Bars were deserted during the middle ages and not developed again until the 19th century. There is at present no evidence for any medieval suburban development outside Newbegin Bar other than the mid 13th-century Franciscan Friary; what happened to the site after the friars had moved to a new position outside Keldgate Bar is not known. In 1416 town rents include rent 'for Aldebeck and waste ground near barredyke near the barre de Newbegin', and closes covering 6 acres outside the bar are mentioned in the late 16th century.[15] The rebuilding of the bar in 1409–10, whether motivated by civic pride or by concern for defence, shows that it was still regarded as a key entrance and, in the 1460 list of bar keepers' fees, that of the keeper of Newbegin Bar is by far the highest.

There is more evidence for medieval settlement and activity outside Keldgate or South Bar. The chapels of St. Helen and St. Thomas were presumably established to serve a community which had grown up during the 13th and 14th centuries around the bar and its approaches from the S. and W. The Greyfriars may have been drawn to Keldgate by the suburb, but the reason for their move in 1297 will probably never be known, and their choice of site may have been determined as much by the availability of land, or by other practical considerations, as by the presence of a poor suburban population in need of ministration. The prebend of St. Michael included lands outside the bar, the site of St. Thomas's chapel among them, and the will of Alan de Humbleton, vicar of St. John's, made in 1329/30, mentions the house in which he lived, its garden, and his grange outside the South Bar.[16]

A century later the suburbs were in decline. The leper house was empty by 1407, in 1434 'diverse tofts containing twelve acres of ground or more, which were late bigged (built upon) and then called Cokwald Strete' had reverted to common land, and 'in the Chapel lane be also diverse tofts containing six acres or more from Keldgate Bar to St. Thomas's chapel which were late bigged'.[17] The main approach roads, however, were still kept in repair. The Town

Keepers' Accounts for 1450/51 record that large quantities of chalk were brought from the quarry in the Westwood to 'the street near the chapel of St. Thomas outside Keldgate bar to mend the causeway there . . . leading from the bar to the Westwood gate . . . near the friars minor', a project important enough to warrant an inspection by nine of the Keepers. It seems likely that this causeway was the raised S. approach from Cottingham and Hessle (Queensgate, first mentioned in 1411, appears more frequently in the records from the late 15th century onwards)[18] rather than the road from the W., which was probably only of local significance; the main approach from this direction passed through Newbegin Bar.

The chalk of Westwood was not only quarried for paving and building but was also used for lime. In 1450/51 John Tasker, lime burner, paid the substantial rent of 53s 4d for the common lime kiln on the Westwood.[19] The kilns 'in le stanpits', mentioned in 1359, were probably lime kilns in the Westwood 'stone pits' rather than tile kilns.[20] Clays are known to have been worked on the common later (in the second decade of the 18th century, for instance, Sir Charles Hotham was permitted to make bricks for his Eastgate House in a corner of the Westwood),[21] but no evidence has been found so far for tile making here in the middle ages, unless the *Aldebeck* near Newbegin is the same as that mentioned in connection with a tilery in 1370.[22] The commons of Westwood and Hurn also yielded oaks and faggots, but by the mid 15th century these were supplemented by imports. A local supply of good building timber was a valuable asset and few, if any, of the medieval towns in Humberside were as fortunate in this respect as Beverley; for major construction work in 15th-century Grimsby timber was brought from as far afield as Balne near Doncaster, a journey by water of 60 miles or more.[23] Hurn was finally denuded of its oaks in the 18th century.

EASTERN SUBURBS

On the E. side of the town the distinction between urban and suburban development is much less clear; some of the difficulties involved in the location of the E. town boundary have already been mentioned. It seems that the large Dominican Friary precinct occupied an intermediate position with its W. side fronting onto a main town street and its E. side extending into the suburbs. The moated Paradise Garth was just outside the Hellgarth Lane 'urban' boundary, and the Trinities to the N. of the friary probably lay near the edge of the settled area. The friary and the preceptory may have attracted some extra-mural settlement, but the strongest inducement to suburban development would have been the town and its trades, and suburban building was probably concentrated along the lanes which led into Walkergate, Fishmarket and Eastgate. The street pattern here departs from the grid system of the town centre and consists of a series of broad, angular loops. This form, suggesting outward growth, has been largely determined by the low-lying ground and by the presence of the religious houses; the impact of the Dominican Friary is particularly striking. How far this road system was developed in the middle ages is uncertain. *Oswaldgate* or *Hayrer Lane* (the present Wilbert Lane), Trinity Lane and Grovehill Road are medieval streets, and Morton Lane, on the E. side of Walkergate, is probably the Old Newbegin mentioned from the 14th century to the 16th century. Mill Lane and Cherry Tree Lane further E. probably began as lanes to the mills in this area (see p. 33). Although low-lying, none of these roads appears to have shared in the paving schemes of the 14th and 15th centuries, perhaps a further indication of their suburban status.[24]

The Beck was from the commercial point of view the most important of the approaches to Beverley,[25] and there can be little doubt that a sizeable community had grown up within a few decades of the completion of the canal, a project probably undertaken at about the time of the town's full evolution to borough status in the early 12th century. The chapel which preceded the parish church of St. Nicholas may have been founded at about the same time and by *c.* 1160 had its own priest. The evolution of the church and churchyard during the 14th and 15th centuries and its subsequent post-Reformation decay reflect the changing fortunes of the town in general, and of Beckside in particular. However, the continuing importance of the Beck as a port protected the area from a decline as severe as that experienced by the W. suburbs.

The town keepers were clearly anxious to keep the waterway and its main approaches in good repair. Pavage tolls collected at the Beck are recorded in their accounts and Henry VI's charter of 1424 confirmed the right to levy tolls on every vessel coming to the town by water, laden with goods for sale.[26] In 1438 the Keepers granted land to John Ousterby on condition that he kept the banks and ditches of the Beck in repair, and four years later three tilemakers paid to remove sixteen boatloads of earth from the N. bank of the canal.[27] In 1454 John Cargrave, a walker, was commissioned 'to finish a pair of cloughs at High Bridge . . . and to scour the Beck from Parson Bridge to St. John House . . . and to cleanse and cut the banks from St. John to the end of the beck'; he was also 'to have the power to stop the Walkerbeck for the weal of the beck'.[28] The High Bridge, which crossed the Beck about 73m. downstream from Low Bridge, where the Walkerbeck joined the Beck, was repaired in 1409 and demolished in 1729, its materials being used to repair Low Bridge (earlier known as Parson's or Little Bridge). The S. side projection was not taken down until 1775.[29] Nothing more is known about St. John House, which was evidently on the Beckside. Its site may be represented by the 'well preserved and finely tooled remains of the early Gothic period' found while digging the sewerage beds on the S. side of the Beck in 1888 (centred on TA 05093922, approximately midway between Low Bridge and the River Hull).[30] The problem of silting seems to have become acute in the 16th century, since considerable sums were collected towards scouring the Beck in 1545 and 1562.[31]

The relative age and importance of the various roads and paths converging on the head of the Beck cannot be determined with any certainty, but it is likely that the basic focal pattern was already established at an early stage. Flemingate, Barleyholme and Aldgate were paved in 1344 and further works were undertaken in Aldgate in the 15th century, including the building of a timber bar, perhaps to control access to Beckside and/or Flemingate. Although Aldgate has yet to be identified, it almost certainly lay in the area of Potter Hill and Beckside. Noutbrig, a bridge repaired in 1449/50, was 'at the end of Aldgate next to Littillund'; the Lund pasture lay S.E. of Beckside on the road from Figham to Hull. The 15th-century rental of the Provostry mentions a number of properties at Beckside.[32] These include a house next to *Ragbrukemyln* and a lane leading to it, a croft between the cemetery of St. Nicholas' church and a lane leading from *Parson Bridge* to the church (the forerunner of Blucher Lane?), houses at *le Bekhead*, at the end of *Parsonbryge* and at the corner of *Holmkyrklane*, a capital messuage called *Quynsmershall*, a tilery 'next to le Beke', and fields called *Heryngcroft*, *Hallecroft* and *Provostengs*. *Guchemerelane*, mentioned in 1461, may have been the early name for Taylor Lane, running from Beckside North to Holme Church Lane. Meaux Abbey sold houses on the *Ragbrook* near the Beck Head in 1210, and an Elizabethan grant refers to cottages on the street 'called Southside of the Becke near the Milne Scutte'.[33] From the available evidence it appears that the blocks of properties on either side of the Beck and along Beckside (formerly Barley Holme) are medieval in origin. Those on the N. side of Barley Holme formerly backed on the E. section of the Walkerbeck just above its outfall into the Beck at Parson's Bridge.[34] This street was one of the town wards and it is interesting to note that its 15th-century tax contributions, sometimes included with those from Beckside, are consistently higher than those from neighbouring Flemingate.

Grovehill, which probably served as the chief landing place before the canalisation of the Beck, continued to function as a port throughout the middle ages. In a lawsuit of 1321 between the archbishop and the burgesses of Hull the latter admitted that, although tolls could be taken from boats and small vessels plying in the town of Beverley, no ships or large vessels had approached any nearer to Beverley than a place called *Grevale* (Grovehill).[35] Transport of building materials from Grovehill is mentioned in the 15th-century Minster Fabric Roll, and in 1536 the burgesses reaffirmed that they were to have the appraising of such fuel or victuals 'as shall come to be sold at the Beck called Beverley Beck, or Groval'.[36] Goods landed at Grovehill were probably brought into the town by Grovehill Road or Holme Church Lane (shown on Burrow's map as *Great Groval Lane* and *Little Grovel Lane*). The Keepers' Accounts for 1344 give details of a large-scale road building project undertaken on 'the way of Groval on the Spay', and in 1420 the chaplain at Grovehill and the toll collector at the river were among con-tributors towards the repair of 'the road towards Grovehill'. The references to a chaplain and that in 1398 to two friars 'of Groval' suggests a cha-pel or hermitage here. Witty mentions 'certain worked stones . . . known in the Grovehill dis-trict' but gives no further details, and the finds may have been those referred to above in con-nection with St. John House.[37]

INDUSTRIAL ACTIVITY

Besides playing a vital role as the town's port, medieval Beckside served as a centre for boatbuilding, tile and brick making, potting, and probably for clothmaking, tanning and associated trades. These were primarily drawn to the area by special needs such as the availability of raw materials, good water supplies and transport facilities, although by the later middle ages trades which involved objectionable or dangerous processes, such as tanning, pot burning and tile making, were often restricted to suburban areas.[38] The name *Potterstartlane* and 15th-century ordinances directed at the tilers and boatbuilders show that there were in effect recognizable 'industrial zones'. Many of these trades were concentrated in the Flemingate–Hellgarth area and along the roads and streams converging on the head of the Beck, but there is also evidence for activity further afield, along the Beckside and towards Grovehill. One of the more important industries was brick and tile making.

Tileries were evidently already well estab-lished at Beverley by the mid 14th century, for the 1359 Magna Charta of the Community, a record of customs and assessments 'anciently used in the town' specifically refers to payments due from tilers.[39] Rent from the tilery of *Alde-beck* is mentioned in 1370, and in the late 14th century Beverley bricks and tiles were used for the new town hall at Grimsby.[40] Tilers from Beverley were taking clay from the banks of the Hull in Sutton and Wawne *c.*1385, much to the annoyance of the monks of Meaux.[41] In the early 15th century tileries are recorded at Beckside and by 1578 a 'tylekilne' was situated at Milbeck on the S. side of the Beck. Bricks, usually re-ferred to as 'wall tiles', were made by the tilers, and examples of their work can still be seen in the North Bar and other buildings in the town. Lists of building materials in the Minster Fabric Roll of 1445–6 include thacktiles (roofing tiles), gutter tiles, wall tiles, ridge tiles and squincheon or scutcheon tiles, the later perhaps used for door and window surrounds; all were probably manufactured locally.[42] In 1461 a new ordinance stated that 'on account of the stink, fouling of the air, and destruction of fruit trees, none to make a kiln to burn tiles in or nearer the said town than the kilns are now built'.[43] No medi-eval tileries have yet been identified. Construc-tion work on the Grovehill Industrial Estate in 1979 revealed extensive layers of hand-made tiles near the N. bank of the Beck, but there was no sign of the site where they were pro-duced. Tile kilns in Beverley, perhaps in the Beckside area, are mentioned in mid 18th-cen-tury property transactions; the most recent brick and tile works lay to the N. of the Beck at TA 048395.

The presence of potters in Beverley is attested by the existence of the medieval potters' guild, by street-names and by archaeological ma-terial.[44] *Potterstartlane* seems to have been off Fle-mingate; *Pottergate* and *Potter Lane* (perhaps synonymous) lay further E., at or near Grove-hill. In 1417 Robert Tyrwhitt rented meadow land lying 'to the east of Pottergate up to the moat of the manor of Grovall', and a position between Holme Church Lane or Grovehill Road and the Beck seems likely.[45]

In 1947–8 R. Carr investigated a small recti-linear embanked enclosure at Grovehill which may be linked with the medieval Pottergate or with Potter Lane 'next grovall'. The site lies about 100m. W. of the River Hull and 300m.

N. of the Beck; it is skirted on the W. by an old track from Grovehill to Beckside.[46] A trial trench cut from the northern bank towards the centre passed through a medieval pottery dump. Although no structural features or kilns were found the large amount of pottery and the presence of kiln-wasters point to production close by; the kilns may in fact have been situated on the slightly elevated, drier ground within the banks.

Mr. Carr retained a dozen sherds of which eleven, including one probable kiln-waster, are of a type well known from late 13th to early 14th-century levels in Hull, where it has been named 'orangeware'. Similar pottery has also been located S. of the Humber, for instance at Thornholme Priory, and large quantities were recovered from 12th, 13th and 14th-century levels on the Highgate site in Beverley. The twelfth sherd was 'Humberware' and it is possible that this type was also produced in the area. The bulk of the pottery ('six sacksfull') was deposited at Beverley Museum but cannot now be traced. Fortunately the site remains free from development and further work here should be possible.

Commercial and industrial activities in the Beckside area obviously involved a good deal of marketing. In 1363 one of the town's two butchers' markets was held in Barley Holme, and shops are recorded there in the late 16th century.[47] At Beckside the quayside itself served as a market-place. In 1441 John Baryer was ordered 'to levy ½d from each boat called a cache unloading straw for thatching, peat, hay and other things between the bridges at the torrent to pay for cleaning the market place there' (i.e. the upper quay between Parson's Bridge and High Bridge).[48] An order of 1476 requiring the potters and *crelers* (carriers using baskets) to carry faggots and *astilwode* (kindling ?) on sleds rather than in carts suggests that these bulky goods were landed downstream from High Bridge.[49] Presumably to prevent congestion around the upper quayside market the Keepers in 1461 ordered 'not to have ships, boats or ketches built or repaired on the banks of the great Beck, between Guchmerelane and Parson-brig, without special leave of the Keepers'.[50] The

supervision of traffic and marketing was more of a problem at the Beck than at the other market-places. In 1405 the Keepers announced that 'no burgess or stranger' was to buy or sell 'faggots, astilwode, coals, or other like fuel, or salt' at the Beck before it had been priced by two of their number, and that no one should 'forestall them (the goods), or buy in gross to resell by way of regrating . . . nor buy on the Beck in fraud of the community, saying that he buys elsewhere outside the liberty'.[51] Evasions of toll were common; in 1416, for instance, several salters were fined for selling at a higher price than that appraised, and in 1450/51 fines were imposed on a Snaith keelman who sold faggots outside his boat and on a creeler who carried faggots to Flemingate before they had been priced by the Keepers.[52]

In the Beckside area lay the 13th-century *Rag-brukemyln,* which may have had some connection with the Low Mill, a 16th-century water-mill situated on the Mill Dam Drain S. of the Beck (approx. TA 046391).[53] *Milnebeck* is mentioned in 1202.[54] Other mills occupied similar peripheral locations. The rental in the early 15th-century Provost's Book refers to four at Norwood,[55] of which three were close to Riding Field on the E. side of the town. The first lay in *Palmerscroft*, the second was called *Trinity Mill,* and the third, belonging to the Knights Hospitallers, was associated with a small house in the N. angle of a close, very near the gate into Riding Field. One of the four may have been the predecessor of the Elizabethan Norwood Mill[56]. On the Westwood there were five mills in the post-medieval period, of which the oldest appears to have been *Westwood Hither Mill* or *Low Mill,* first mentioned in 1650, but possibly much older.[57] Medieval and later mills within the built-up area were invariably powered by horses. In 1329 John de Bridlington is mentioned in connection with rent for land with a horse mill on it in Dead Lane, next to St. Mary's churchyard.[58] Water-powered fulling-mills were introduced into Britain in the 12th century and spread rapidly, but there is no evidence that such mills operated at Beverley, where the fulling process was carried out by the walkers who trampled and beat the damp cloth until the wool fibres had adequately felted.

MOATED SITES

Four moated sites lay close to the medieval borough but outside the built-up area. Two of these (Woodhall and Pighill) are now incorporated in the town's suburbs. Other earthworks, some of which may represent the remains of medieval enclosures, are described below in the section on commons.

A moated site belonging to Woodhall Manor is mentioned from the early 14th century onwards. Excavations by W. J. Varley in 1965–7 sectioned the moat (TA 02544110), which was of medieval origin and 3 ft. (0.9m.) deep, and uncovered a rectangular granary or aisled barn with an annexe and chalk-cobbled floor, a stackyard and a roadway.[59] The central platform contained buildings of four phases but only the foundations of their supports had survived. To the S. lay three fishponds, of which the largest, together with the moat, revealed two phases of occupation, each followed by a period of abandonment. The earliest pottery was dated to the late 13th century and occupation apparently ceased in the 15th century. The finds and some plans are in Hull Museum. In 1824 foundations, 'ancient smooth wall tiles' and two Roman coins were found at the end of Pighill Lane (Woodhall Way). Although Oliver associated these remains with *Estoft*, the location given rather suggests that they occurred on or very close to the Woodhall moat.[60]

Another moated site, part of which survives, lies on the E. side of Pighill Lane at TA 03024046. It may have contained the residence of the Copandale family in the 14th century, although that may have been in Norwood.[61] A further moated enclosure on the N. side of the town is marked on the O.S. 6in. map of 1885 to the S. of Scrubwood Lane and W. of the railway line which bisects the site (TA 03684124). This may have been the capital messuage known as *Estoft*, held in Henry VI's reign by John Bedford, which lay near Woodhall.[62]

The 'moat of the manor of Grovall' mentioned in the early 15th-century Provost's Book (see p. 32) lay between Pottergate and the River Hull, probably in the area now cut by the Beverley and Barmston Drain and partly occupied by commercial buildings (centred on TA 054395).

SANCTUARY CROSSES

Throughout the middle ages Beverley was ringed with a line of sanctuary crosses, described by Folcard and later writers, which defined the triple limits of the sanctuary (Fig. 2).[63] Of these only three survive, at Bishop Burton (TA 005397), at Walkington (TA 004374) and at Bentley (TA 026364). There was originally also one at Molescroft, mentioned by Alured of Beverley, but apparently not surviving later than the middle ages. According to Poulson it was 'in a valley a little beyond the hamlet' and a position on the Malton road seems likely. The sanctuary was traditionally granted by King Athelstan and was confirmed by Stephen in 1136 as Athelstan's gift; it was abolished in the 16th century.[64] The cross at Bishop Burton had an inscription still legible in the 18th century.[65] All three remaining crosses may have been moved from their original sites as the distances between their present locations and those recorded in earlier documents seem more than usually discrepant.

COMMONS

The medieval borough's common lands comprised Westwood and Hurn (effectively one unit), Figang (Figham) with Lund, Swinemoor, and the Tonge, altogether amounting to over 1200 acres.[66] Archbishop Sewall de Boville granted to the borough rights of common in Figham *c.* 1258 and at about the same time the burgesses surrendered their rights in the archbishop's park S. of the town (Beverley Parks) in exchange for certain rights on the Westwood. A further agreement was made in 1282, and in 1379–80 Archbishop Alexander Neville granted to the Town Keepers and burgesses 'un boys appelle le Westwood de Beverlee' in return for an annual rent of 100*s.*, which was paid until 1543 when the archbishop surrendered his land and manorial rights in Beverley to the Crown. The origins of the borough's rights of common on Swinemoor are not known; MacMahon suggests that the burgesses had secured rights there by the 14th century. The Tonge, a pasture at the end of the Beck, was held by the town until 1501, when it was granted by the Keepers to Edward Minskip in part exchange for his messuage in the Cross Garths (see p. 55). Prior to 18th and 19th-century drainage schemes large areas of the eastern pastures must have been flooded during the winter months. Stephenson records that as late as the early 19th century small flat-bottomed boats could come along the dikes as far as Norwood.[67]

Westwood, Swine Moor and Figham contain earthworks which seem to be mainly medieval or later in date.[68] On Westwood a bank and ditch extend from TA 01403892 to TA 02133912 with a break at TA 01793922. The western length runs parallel to and S. of the North Newbald Road (the N. side of the road is also flanked by a linear work set back some distance from it). The eastern length runs up the side of a dry valley and zig-zags to the wold top near the Black Mill; it may be a hollow way or a boundary. Hollow ways or sunken trackways form a prominent feature of the Westwood and chiefly occur at the following locations: N. of North Newbald Road (TA 01363934, 01593907); S. of North Newbald Road (TA 01903930, 02253953, 01573889, 01633884); midway between North Newbald Road and Walkington Road (TA 01763876); near Walkington Road (TA 02533925 and 02273875); near Keldgate Road (TA 02673883); and near the path, Gilly Croft Trod (TA 02783912). Two parallel marks 20m. apart at TA 02183886, visible on air photographs, may indicate another former road (between Walkington Road and the Black Mill). Just N. of the York Road, at TA 02553975, part of an early arable field survives in the form of ridge and furrow. In addition there are several ponds, now largely dry, and extensive pits, hollows and hillocks as evidence of the widespread exploitation of the chalk and clay of Westwood during the medieval and post-medieval periods.

In addition to these medieval and later remains some earthworks on the Westwood may be Iron Age or Roman in date. In Burton Bushes a rectilinear enclosure is visible at the crossing of two woodland rides. The enclosure measures 46m. by 34m. overall and is defined by a bank 6m. wide and 0.4m. high with an outer ditch 4.5m. wide and 0.3m. deep; it may have been for livestock or for settlement. Marks on air photographs suggest that other rectilinear enclosures to the E. at TA 01403948 may have been levelled by ploughing. Nearby, at TA 01553885, earthworks, together with a bulge to the W. in the parish boundary with Bishop Burton, suggest a large enclosure 130m. by 50–100m. defined by a bank and outer ditch. To the N.E. of these are hollow ways and natural ridges, which from the air look like further enclosures.

Roughly in the centre of Swine Moor at TA 05004085 are two enclosures delineated by banks and ditches; the larger has mature trees growing on the bank. Near the Beverley and Barmston Drain at TA 05294066 is a long mound flanked by ditches. A number of tracks cross the moor, in places flanked by side ditches; the most prominent is a raised road at TA 04824112, possibly made in 1773.[69] To the S. of it lies an E.N.E. to W.S.W. ditch which has a small rectangular enclosure attached to it on the S. side at TA 04634098; at the W. end the ditch may be overlaid with ridge and furrow (TA 04524099).

The site of Swine Moor Wells lies towards the northern edge of the moor at TA 05084119. Water from the spring, dedicated to St. John of Beverley, was formerly drunk for medicinal purposes and from about 1700 to 1815 was also used for bathing. The spa house, built in 1747, was demolished in 1955.[70] The site is now a hedged enclosure, partly surrounded by a water-filled ditch, containing a building platform with a large hollow at one end. A small depression near the hedge may represent one of the wells. Just outside the enclosure on the S. is a scatter of glass and pottery of 18th and 19th-century date.

On Figham occur former field boundaries which in places are fairly substantial, especially near Figham Clough Bridge at TA 05883879. Ridge and furrow is visible nearby at TA 05753870.

Notes

1 For a discussion of medieval suburbs see D. J. Keene in Barley, 71–82, and Platt, 38–40.
2 In 1520/21 common expenses include 'alms to divers poor infected in this great sickness (*infirmitate*)' in the wholly, or predominantly, suburban areas of 'Beckside, Kelgate, Kyrklane (Holme Church Lane) and outside North Bar' (HMC, 173).
3 Examples of tax lists are given in HMC, 57, 112, 126, 137 and 45. The list of wards varies; those given here occur most regularly.
4 Leach 1903, 316–17.
5 For examples of subscription lists see HMC, 106, 116–17, 134, 140.
6 BBR Town Keepers' Account Roll 1450/51.
7 HMC, 123; Poulson, Appendix 32, 33, 40, 43. The 1438 entry is in HMC, 121.
8 *BG*, 17. Jan. 1857.
9 Hebditch, 23; Poulson, App. 35.
10 Plan of Beverley by John Wood, 1828.
11 Leach 1903, 318–19.
12 Witty, *BG*, 16 Aug. 1930; Leach 1900, 48.
13 e.g. in 1726: HCRO Registry of Deeds 1 386/848.
14 Brown 1973, 10; Witty, op. cit. in n.12.
15 BBR Town Keepers' Account Roll 1416; Poulson, App. 36.
16 See Leach 1903, 335 and Hebditch, 13–15.
17 HMC, 22.
18 The *Queenstreet* recorded in an Elizabethan grant (Poulson, App. 43) lay near the North Bar and may have been the main thoroughfare, North Bar Within-Without.
19 BBR Town Keepers' Accounts 1450/51.
20 HMC, 15; the entry is distinct from that for the tilers' furnaces.
21 MacMahon 1973, 52.
22 See below, p. 32 for tile kilns in the Beckside area.
23 Gillett, 3.
24 Old Newbegin or *Aldnewebygyng* appears to have joined Walkergate N. of Oswaldgate (Poulson, App. 33, 38), though Witty places it between Hengate and Walkergate (*BG*, 15 Feb. 1930). De Boer suggests that this was the Newbegin mentioned in 1190, becoming Old Newbegin due to the creation of a new Newbegin near Lairgate in the 14th century (de Boer, 29, 56). Another possibility is that the 12th-century name records new building in the town centre following the fire of 1188.
25 *Transport History* 4 (1971), 122, 137; MacMahon 1973, 57–8.
26 e.g. HMC, 118, 120. See also Witty, *BG*, 25 Jan. 1930.
27 Witty, op. cit. in n. 26; HMC, 129–30; the entry relating to William Chetil indicates that a *cache*-load is equivalent to five chaldrons of coal.
28 HMC, 11.
29 MacMahon 1973, 57; MacMahon 1958, 14; HMC, 103, 158.
30 *BI*, 9 June 1888.
31 HMC, 176, 181, 182.
32 Leach 1903, 313–16.
33 Bond I, 314; Poulson, App. 44; see also Leach 1898, 99.
34 See p. 18 and n. 11, p. 26.
35 Quoted by Witty, op. cit. in n. 26, giving as a reference *Hargraves Law Tracts*, 70.
36 Leach 1899, 59; HMC, 55.
37 BBR Town Keepers' Account Roll 1344; Witty, op. cit. in n. 26; HMC, 146. There was a chapel of St. James at Hull Bridge (TA 055417), mentioned in a 13th-century deed and in Henry VI's reign; a hermit house probably stood nearby (Hebditch, 11; HMC, 122; Poulson, 117, 131, 170, 791; Oliver, 330).
38 In the late 18th century most of the town's tanners were in the Beckside – Barleyholme – Flemingate area. Others operated in Keldgate, Lairgate, North Bar Without, Walkergate, and Toll Gavel (Witty, *BG*, 14 Dec. 1929). It seems likely that their late medieval predecessors occupied similarly peripheral sites.
39 HMC, 14–15.
40 Leach 1903, 315; HMC, 62; Dennett, 41; Gillett, 2.
41 Bond III, 179–181.
42 Leach 1899, 54–5, 60–1. 'Squincheon' tiles appear as *qwynshontylle* and *squynshontiell*.
43 HMC, 48.
44 HMC, 69. In 1662/3 permission was given to two persons to dig clay in Swinemoor for making pots (Dennett, 129), but revoked in 1665.
45 Witty, *BG*, 26 Oct. 1929; Leach 1903, 320.
46 Information from Mr. R. Carr, who loaned pottery from the excavation to the Humberside Archaeological Unit.
47 HMC, 103; Poulson, App. 37.
48 HMC, 126.
49 HMC, 102–3.
50 HMC, 48.
51 HMC, 70.

52 HMC, 159; BBR Town Keepers' Account Roll 1450/ 51.

53 MacMahon 1958, 4, 148; Leach 1903, 313, 314; Poulson, 628 n. 1.

54 Brown 1894, 43.

55 Leach 1903, 319, 320; Oliver, 297 n. 77.

56 Poulson, App. 29; Oliver, 285.

57 Other Westwood mills have a later origin. The mills, some of which still partially survive, were situated at TA 02233917 (Hither), 02093898 (High), 02193852 (Union), 02793921 (Butt Close) and 02723862 (Dowson's). See BDCS, section 2.

58 *CPR 1327–30*, 405.

59 YASRS 16 (1894), 131; *ERA* 2 (1975), 12–45; *YAJ* 42 (1970), 388; *Med. Arch.* 10 (1966), 205; 14 (1970), 195; O.S. 1:10,560 map (1855).

60 Oliver, 511.

61 Allen, 187; Oliver, 285; Sheahan and Whellan, 227.

62 Oliver, 511.

63 Raine 1879, 297–8; *Sanctuarium Dunelmense et Sanctuarium Beverlacense*, Surtees Soc. 5. (1837), 99; Forster and Brown, 18, pl. XV. A recent summary is Kirby, R. M., 'Sanctuary and Sanctuary Crosses', BDCS Newsletter 44 (Winter 1980) and 45 (Spring 1981).

64 Farrer, 93–4.

65 Poulson, 687 and pl.

66 MacMahon 1973, 17–19.

67 Stephenson, 272.

68 Information from RCHM (E), York. Further details are noted in the Commission's record cards and air photographs.

69 MacMahon 1958, 52.

70 Dennett, 173, 191; MacMahon 1958, xx, 23, 60.

PLATE 3.   North Bar from the N. A late 18th-century sketch.

THE DEFENCES

Surrounding much of the medieval town were defences, the nature of which has been much debated.[1] The town ditch *(barredic)* is first mentioned in the mid 12th century, soon after Beverley had achieved full borough status. In the 15th century the name 'Bar Dike', though later given to a pond outside the North Bar, clearly referred to the W. section of the town ditch, the line of which was certainly established by the mid 13th century.[2] There is no clear topographical evidence for an earlier defensive circuit, but without excavation it is impossible to be sure that the later bar dike followed the same course as the 12th-century ditch. In 1321–2 a petition to the King asked that the burgesses 'be allowed to enclose the town with a wall and ditch', but his final answer is unknown.[3] In 1376 a commission of array referred to the 'defect of the fortifications', but these were not described in any detail.[4] Unlike Hull or York, Beverley received no grants of murage (the right to levy tolls for defensive works) and 14th-century sources refer only to the gates and ditch. Leland 'could not percyve that ever hit was waulled' and it seems likely that the town was encircled only by a palisaded earth bank with an external ditch.[5]

The town had four main gates or Bars, augmented in the 15th century by a series of lesser bars and turnstiles, documentary evidence for which has come to light during this survey. In addition to the maintenance costs for North Bar, Norwood Bar, Keldgate or South Bar and Newbegin Bar, the Town Keepers' accounts include the costs of building, repairing and keeping a number of other bars, turnstiles and minor defensive works, some obviously only temporary structures. Although many of the sites named cannot be accurately identified, the records show that the provision of entry points on the E. side of the town was more flexible than on the N. and W. where the defensive circuit was more clearly defined. Apparently the town had partly outgrown its earlier eastern boundary but, instead of replacing it with a new defensive earthwork, the Keepers relied on a series of street barriers and timber bars. The entries in their accounts are summarised below in chronological order, omitting costs of repairs to the main bars.

In 1391 'a chain in Flemingate, having 50 links', perhaps for toll purposes, was handed over to the Keepers, along with others at the Beck of 52 links, at North Bar of 44 links, and 'two lying in the Guildhall' of 36 and 26 links.[6] In 1405 a whole entry was devoted to the costs of a new bar; this was probably not North Bar, repaired in the same year, but perhaps one of the others rebuilt in brick and stone (Keldgate Bar?).[7]

The accounts for 1445 give the costs of works on five wooden bars and two turnstiles, including the carriage of wood to the guildhall, work on a bar 'at the end of the town lane', and payments for two bars in *Aldnewebyging* and *Estgate*.[8] More timber was brought to make a bar at the end of *Bradwellane* and two carpenters were paid for work on 'the bar newly built between the friars preachers (i.e. the Blackfriars) and Helgarth'. The turnstiles were sited at the end of *Seyngelylane* (St. Giles Lane) and in *Wodlane;* faggots were brought from Westwood to roof three earth walls built at the ends of *Dedlane, Paynlane* and *Frerelane.* A separate entry is concerned with the cost of defending the town 'against the malice of Mathew Hoggeson, Henry de Seler, William de Ewery and other evildoers, their associates'. This includes keeping the four main gates and a bar at the end of Trinity Lane next to Eastgate.

Under the heading 'costs of the gates of the town' the accounts for 1450/51 include details of work 'on the bar newly made in Aldgate near the torrent' (probably the Beck or the Walkerbeck).[9] Oaks and spars were brought for this work and two labourers were employed to dig 'foundations in the earth for the posts of the said bar.'; an iron chain, staple and *platelok* were bought for locking the bar. The oaks were brought from Westwood to the guildhall, perhaps to check or store the materials before use, or because the bar was situated nearby, in the Walkergate area. However, the evidence suggests that Aldgate was in the S.E. part of the town, since in a street paving account of 1344 it is included with Flemingate and Barleyholme. In 1444 further repairs in Aldgate include 'making bars beside Hellegarthes', presumably the 'Railles' in this street mended in 1545/6.[10]

From 1449/50 the accounts begin to include the fees of the bar keepers. In 1449/50 the keepers of North Bar and Norwood Bar are mentioned.[11] In 1450/51 the keepers' fees perhaps indicate the status of each bar: Norwode bar 2s; North Bar 3s 4d; Newbigyng bar 2s; Keldgate bar 2s 4d; Aldnewbigyng 8d.[12] In 1460 the list runs: gate at North Bar 2s; bar of Newbigyng 3s 4d; bar of Norewod 2s; South bar 2s; bar at Belmanlane 12d.[13]

The defensive ditch ran E. from North Bar along the S. side of Wylies Road and then turned S. along Manor Road to Norwood Bar. Its alignment beyond this point is uncertain, though Walkergate may mark its continuation to skirt Wednesday Market and Eastgate. It may then have continued S. past the Minster Yard or E. to enclose Flemingate. To the S. of the Minster Hall Garth may have formed an enclosure within the ditch or the moat itself served as part of the defences. The borough boundary follows the Mill Dam drain for much of the S. section, but turns N. around Hall Garth, excluding from the borough the moat and the area to the S. of it, still part of Woodmansey and the rural parish of St. John's rather than of the town parish of St. Martin's. To the W. of Hall Garth the ditch swung N.W. through the present allotments S. of Keldgate and then ran N. from Keldgate Bar through the Leases and by Newbegin Bar to turn E. for a short distance back to North Bar. The remains of the defences are described below in detail because the evidence of their course and nature has not previously been published.

The North Bar (TA 03003988) was the principal entry to Beverley. Mentioned in the late 13th century[14] and repaired in 1405, it was rebuilt in local brick in 1409–10 at a cost of £96.0s 11½d and still exists, the earliest surviving brick gateway of its type in the country (Plate 3).[15] The bricks are of a size and bonding similar to brickwork in the Minster nave vault but the bonding now seems irregular, maybe due to frequent patching and repair. The Bar has simply moulded bricks for the hoodmould, a cornice of a type which lasted in use until the late 18th century, and shaped bricks for arches, cusps and finials. The cornice has projecting courses sandwiching one row of bricks laid diagonally so as to expose one corner of each brick. It is rib-vaulted inside, has a portcullis slot and retains its later wooden gates. In 1450/51 Roger Cokirham, a mercer, paid rent for a town house on the W. side of the Bar and the 'chamber over the Bar'.[16] The E. passageway was created in 1793–4 (p. 54), and construction work on the W. passageway in 1867 uncovered an extremely thick stone wall thought to have been part of an earlier gateway structure.

To the E. of North Bar the ditch is represented by a change in ground level between Garden Cottage and the County Council office car park S. of Wylies Road (TA 03033992 – 03073995). The grounds of Garden Cottage lie about lm. lower than those of its S. neighbour, Bar Chambers. In the children's playground to the E. the change in level takes the form of a gentle N.-facing slope 10–12m. wide, beyond which the ground dips slightly to the S. This may represent the S. side of the town ditch and spread remains of a bank or merely be the results of modern disturbance. Early O.S. maps mark the site of the ditch either along Wylies Road (1854 1:1056 edition) or on its S. side (1892 1:500 map) and continuing round into Pighill Lane (now Manor Road) towards Norwood Bar. The ditch here carried the Walkerbeck or an existing watercourse was adopted as the town ditch. The Pighill Lane section of the beck was covered in 1826. The culvert, now beneath the central reservation of the dual carriageway, was exposed in 1971, but no archaeological record was made.

Norwood Bar (TA 03353986 ?) is mentioned several times in the 15th century but had disappeared by Leland's time. It is thought to have stood at the E. end of Hengate, two stone posts marking the spot in the early 19th century.

The Walkerbeck probably served as the town ditch S. of this bar. Walkergate, which follows the beck, truncates the cross streets and defines the E. limit of the associated burgage blocks which extend from Saturday Market. In 1405 repairs were carried out on 'the torrent' (probably this beck) and to 'le Bek'; 'a block of wood . . . 900 bricks and 4 quarters of stone' were also bought for 'the bridge at the end of Bowbriglane' which spanned the Walkerbeck.[17] A paving account of 1443 includes an entry for 4000 bricks to 'make the banks of the torrent in Walkergate', a more 'urban' treatment than that undertaken farther N., where, in 1445, the bank was made 'with faggots from the Westwood' as part of a scheme of work on *Netbrig* near Norwood. In 1450/51 a bridge was made 'over the Walkerbeck opposite the Gild Hall' in Walkergate. The scale and nature of these improvements suggest that by the mid 15th century the built-up area had spread to the E. side of the beck. Development in this area, perhaps associated with cloth manufacture alongside the beck, may already have been under way in the early 14th century, for Oswaldgate and Walkergate are mentioned in 1327 and the latter was paved

in 1344, along with the town's other main streets. The brick conduit on the W. side of Walkergate, rebuilt in the 1890s, was exposed in 1971 and 1978, unfortunately without archaeological record, since the relationship between medieval Walkergate and the beck bears directly on the question of medieval urban limits and the nature of the E. town boundary.[18]

The course of the town ditch and the limits of medieval urban development are even more uncertain further S. It may have run along Butcher Row and Wednesday Market to the Trinity Lane – Eastgate junction (the site of a 15th-century bar), and then continued down Eastgate to the Minster Yard. Such a line would imply a major reorganisation of the early medieval settlement, for it would have excluded not only land on the E. side of the thoroughfare through Wednesday Market and Butcher Row, but also the presumed area of early settlement on the E. side of Eastgate and along Flemingate. The effect would have been to channel development towards the N., which may tie in with the shift of urban focus which appears to have taken place in the 12th and 13th centuries. However, there is at present no firm evidence for a ditch along Eastgate and the possibility of a line further E. must be considered.

The presence of St. John the Baptist's Hospital and of burgage plots and timber-framed houses on the E. side of Butcher Row and Wednesday Market show that, at least in the later medieval period, the properties along this frontage formed part of the town proper. Early maps suggest that the 'urban' boundary here ran behind the plots to a point near the junction of Trinity Lane and Grovehill Road. This may represent an earlier boundary which had continued S. behind the plots on the E. side of Eastgate before the creation of the Dominican Friary precinct.[19] The substantial N.–S. drain (Oliver refers to a 'moat')[20] which passes under the E. wing of the surviving friary building might represent the line of a (town ?) boundary ditch antedating the friary foundation. Nineteenth-century maps suggest that this drain was continued S.E. by a broad ditch alongside Hellgarth Lane. In 1448 the Keepers granted to Ralph Sutor, tanner, 'the use and right of way of a bridge over the public fosse for coming and going to the lands of Thomas Lydall near the friars preachers',[21] and it was here, 'between the friars preachers and Helgarth', that a bar was newly built in 1445.[22]

Flemingate formed an integral part of medieval Beverley and it seems reasonable to suppose that at least part of this E. arm of the town was included within the defences. The earliest maps suggest that Hellgarth Lane demarcated the N. margin of the urban settlement here. The lane, now largely obscured by modern industrial development, previously followed the rear boundaries of the strip plots fronting on Flemingate, dividing them from an area of small fields to the N. where the plot pattern was suburban in character. Wood's survey of 1828 and the O.S. map of 1854 show an intermittent water-filled ditch up to about 2–3m. wide along the S. side of the road, possibly representing the course of a former town ditch.[23] On the S. side of Flemingate the evidence is less straightforward. An irregular boundary marks the transition from urban plots to fields,[24] and 150–200m. S. of this lies the substantial Mill Dam Drain, followed by the borough and parish boundaries, which could have served as an effective town defence. It is clear from the Keepers' paving accounts and from the list of porters' and creelers' carriage charges that Flemingate was the official route between Beckside and the town, and as such may have been controlled by a bar or toll gate.[25] There is no evidence for a bar in the street, but the Ordnance Survey's note of the supposed site of the South Bar on Potter Hill was possibly based on a tradition or other evidence of a bar controlling access along Flemingate.

The line of any defence on the S. side of Beverley is uncertain. However to the S.W. part of an infilled ditch was revealed at the junction of Minster Avenue and Long Lane in excavations for the Beverley High Level Sewer in April 1980. The possibility that this represents the town ditch is strengthened by evidence from Long Lane, where the medieval road surface N. of ('inside') the ditch had been built up with layers of timber and chalk, but there was no sign of such 'paving' on the S. side. On the same alignment is an E.–W. bank and infilled ditch in the grounds of Keldgate Manor which aligns with the S. garden fence of 40 Long Lane

(TA 03613897 – 03703900). In the tanyard to the W. short sections of ditches are shown on the 1892 plan, and a water-filled ditch on the E. side of Kitchen Lane may continue the line from there past Bleach Yard Cottages (TA 03523892 – 03413888). From the W. side of the lane to TA 03343890 the line is represented by a wet ditch about 1m. wide running through the allotments; the O.S. plan of 1892 shows a ditch here up to 5m. wide tailing away to the S. Burrow's map shows a continuous property boundary between Kitchen Lane and Humber Street (Queensgate), now interrupted by the allotments. From the W. side of these a broad shallow depression followed by a property boundary runs to the rear of the former almshouses, 165–9 Keldgate (TA 03293892 – 03193898).

Keldgate Bar (TA 03193901) was repaired in 1386, and in 1450 William Morthwayt, who rented the chamber over the bar and an adjacent piece of land, 'roofed and repaired the said chamber'.[26] It was again repaired in 1643 as part of defensive measures during the Civil War. The bar (Plate 4) was demolished in 1808 and in 1882 the laying of water pipes exposed its foundations. The name Southbargate occurs as early as *c.* 1250, property outside the South Bar is mentioned in a will of 1329/30,[27] and in 1344 the bar was repaired with timber after being damaged by a cart.[28] Although previous writers have regarded the South Bar as a fifth main entrance to the town and suggested a number of sites, recent research has revealed that South Bar was another name for Keldgate Bar.[29] In 14th-century wills the site of the leper house is described either as outside Keldgate Bar or outside the South Bar.[30] In the Keepers' Accounts for 1445 the cost of keeping Keldgate Bar is listed but there is no entry for the South Bar, while in 1460 the reverse is true.

The Keepers' Accounts for 1405 mention a watering place at Keldgate near the Minster and another near Norwood is mentioned in 1445. It looks as though the town ditch or its tributary streams formed pools at these places. In 1450 labourers were paid for 'clearing willow this year . . . in Bardike near the Friars Minor' (i.e. the second Franciscan Friary site outside Keld-

PLATE 4. Keldgate Bar from the W., from a watercolour.

gate Bar; and 'for planting *dez Settyngez* on both sides of the spring'.[31] Whether this spring was associated with the town ditch is not apparent; the 'quickfall' on its banks was protected by an enclosure of faggots brought from the lime pits on the Westwood. Rent for the Keldgate bar dike was still being paid to the Keepers in 1556.

The O.S. 1:1056 map of 1853 shows a water-filled ditch between Keldgate and the present junction of St. Giles Croft and the Leases. The S. portion survived to 1928, when it was levelled prior to road construction. The O.S.1:500 plan of 1892 shows the earthworks of this section most clearly: a water-filled ditch 5–7m. wide, accompanied for most of its length by an internal bank (in the N. by a slight external bank), ran from Keldgate to the present junction of Champney Road with the Leases. These earthworks (Map 1) no doubt incorporate alterations made during the Civil War, when

the ditch was widened, and were part of drainage and garden schemes in the 18th and 19th centuries.[32] To the N. of St. Giles Croft the E. arm of the rampart which enclosed the mid 13th-century Franciscan Friary ran parallel to the ditch. This section, now occupied by Albert Terrace (formerly Slut Well Lane), was already levelled by the mid 19th century. Drainage excavations here in 1889 revealed the ditch near the end of Grayburn Lane (formerly Cattfosse Lane), where it was said to be 7–8 yds. wide.

Newbegin Bar (TA 03023952) was rebuilt in 1409–10, repaired in 1643 and finally demolished in 1790. MacMahon suggests that the rebuilding of this and of the North Bar were 'the beginnings of a belated attempt, with royal approval, to strengthen the site of the town, following the unsuccessful rebellion of the Percies . . . in 1408'.[33] The length of walling on the N. side of this bar shown in a 19th-century print (Plate 5) suggests that more substantial defences were intended but never completed.

Further N. short sections of the ditch survive as a broad shallow depression in the gardens behind 1 Woodlands – 60 Wood Lane (TA 02963965) and in the garden of St. Mary's Vicarage (TA 02933970). Even where the ditch itself is not visible much of its line can be traced in the pattern of streets and property boundaries. Those E.–W. cross streets which formerly terminated on the ditch, like Tiger Lane and Wood Lane, reveal its position by a kink or change in width. Others run outside the ditch (Quaker Lane) or along it (Albert Terrace and the Leases). At the N.W. angle the ditch turned E. to North Bar, outside which was a large pool known in the post-medieval period as the Cuckstoolpit or the Bar Dike and filled in 1867.[34] On Burrow's map (Fig. 4) the pool joins the long, narrow pond or dike known as Willow Row. In the Middle Ages the Willow Row springs would have fed the W. ditch and perhaps the N. ditch as well, for Stephenson reported that its water 'finds its way into the Walkerbeck'.[35] Drainage excavations outside the North Bar in 1889 uncovered what was thought to be the town ditch, together with coins, bones and timber.[36]

PLATE 5.   Newbegin Bar from the W., after *Sketches*, 1882.

Notes

1 Allen, 166, 187–8; Poulson, 95, 96, 115, 131, 191–2, 209–10; Oliver, 163–5; Sheahan and Whellan, 189–91; Clay, 21–3, 27–8; MacMahon 1958, 16, 74, 97, 143; HMC, 157, 158; Bilson 1896; *Sketches*; *BG*, 18 Feb. 1882; 5 Sept. 1929; *BI*, 2 Feb. 1889.

2 Smith, 196. Note also the Burdike at Grimsby (Gillett, 2, 13, 75) and the Bardyke at Boston (Harden, 18–20), both consisting of a bank and ditch.

3 MacMahon 1973, 17.

4 *CPR* 1370–74, 101.

5 Leland, v, 39.

6 HMC, 71–2.

7 BBR Town Keepers' Account Roll 1405.

8 ibid., 1445.

9 ibid., 1450/51.

10 ibid., 1444; 1545/6.

11 ibid., 1449/50.

12 ibid., 1450/51.

13 ibid., 1460.

14 National Register of Archives Report, Spencer Stanhope MSS No. 4.

15 Bilson 1896; Leach 1896.

16 BBR Town Keepers' Account Roll 1450/51.

17 ibid., 1405; a bridge had been built here in 1344 (ibid., 1344). See Witty, *BG*, 12 Oct. 1929.

18 Although the Walkerbeck is often referred to in medieval records as the 'common ditch', its public character is not necessarily proof of a status as the town ditch. The section of it S. of Cross Bridge, through an area certainly well within the town centre, was also known as the 'common ditch' or 'sewer', as it was N. of Barley Holme (BBR Schedules III/13, III/2, III/3; see also notes 11 and 34, pp. 26, 36).

19 A common sewer bordering the E. side of Eastgate properties is mentioned in 1440 (Hebditch, 24).

20 Oliver, 276.

21 HMC, 130. The 'Spowte' of the friars mentioned in 1502/3 (HMC, 170) may have had some connection with this watercourse.

22 BBR Town Keepers' Accounts 1445.

23 A common watercourse is mentioned here in 1318 (HMC, 21). In the 19th century the ditch was also known as Shittendike or Tan Dike (Witty, *BG*, 7 Dec. 1929).

24 In the allotments S. of Flemingate a long depression curves N. from Spark Mill Lane towards Potter Hill (TA 04283905 – 04313916). This feature, frequently flooded in wet weather, could represent a former ditch (see Map 1).

25 Paving expenses for Flemingate are mentioned in the Town Keepers' Accounts for 1344, 1366 and 1405 (see also HMC, 128). For porters' and creelers' charges see HMC, 102–3.

26 BBR Town Keepers' Account Roll 1450/51.

27 Hebditch, 13–15.

28 BBR Town Keepers' Account Roll 1344.

29 Witty places it 'to the Minster side of Trinity Lane end, just before Blizzard's Yard end' (the yard of the former George and Dragon), *BG*, 12 Oct. 1929; Stephenson (278) refers to a position 'adjoining Eastgate near Friars Lane'; early O.S. maps mark a site at Potter Hill (TA 04353926). The Minster vicarage's dining room wall (TA 03783932) was also said to have been built on the South Bar's foundations.

30 B.I. Prob. Reg. III, f. 24; ff. 71v–72.

31 BBR Town Keepers' Account Roll 1450/51. Two iron sickles found in the primary silting of the Hall Garth moat during excavation of the bridge abutment (p. 11) had probably been used for clearing the banks.

32 Poulson, 365: '1643, 13th Oct . . . Ordered that a broad ditch be cast at the west end of everie lane leading into Westwood, and only a foot bridge made . . . over such dytches. And . . . that the North bar Newbegin bar and Keldgate bar shall be forthwith put into a state of repair, and shall be kept locked . . . from nine of the clock at night till six of the clock in the morning'. Cf. Stephenson, 278.

33 MacMahon 1973, 17.

34 ibid., 55.

35 Stephenson, 272.

36 *BG*, 11 May 1889.

MEDIEVAL BUILDINGS

In this section the principal buildings of the medieval town other than the Minster, its collegiate buildings, and the gateways of the town defences, already considered, are briefly described. St. Mary's Church and part of the Dominican Friary still stand but the rest are known only from documentary or archaeological evidence. All were public or communal buildings in that they were used for assemblies, whether religious or secular, like the churches, chapels and guildhall, by monastic communities of friars or knights hospitallers, or to shelter the sick and aged inhabitants of Beverley, as with the hospitals and leper-houses. The few surviving medieval private houses are discussed in the following section with the timber-framed buildings of the post-medieval period.

CHURCHES

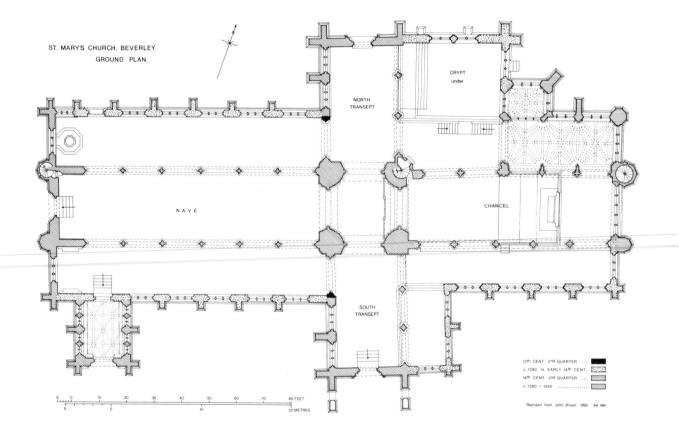

Fig. 8.   St. Mary's Church: ground plan (after Bilson 1920).

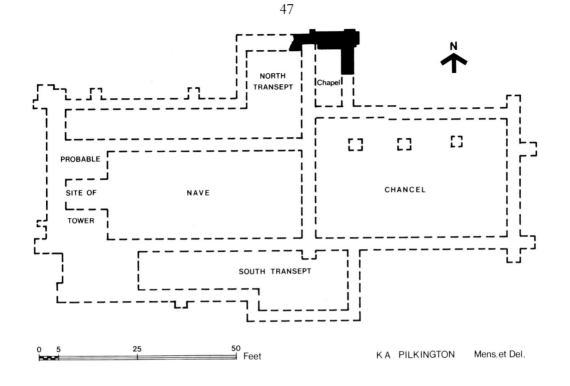

NORTH TRANSEPT

Chapel

N

PROBABLE

SITE OF

TOWER

NAVE

CHANCEL

SOUTH TRANSEPT

0 5   25   50
                            Feet

K A PILKINGTON   Mens. et Del.

Fig. 9. St. Nicholas' Church: plan based on excavations by Carr and MacMahon, 1939.

St. Mary's Church (TA 03153980). A source seen by Leland ascribed the origin of this and of St. Thomas's Chapel to the growth of population in the time of Athelstan, but some have suggested that Archbishop Thurstan (1119–40) was the founder, others that he renewed a ruined Saxon chapel.[1] However, little is known of its history until 1269, when a vicarage was instituted. The plan and architectural features of the present building, analysed in detail by John Bilson, suggest a complicated history, starting in the mid 12th century with a short chancel and an aisleless nave, separated by a tower.[2] The suggested development includes the addition of transepts *c.* 1200, then of aisles, first to the nave and subsequently to the transepts and chancel, the provision of a clerestory and of a turretted W. front *c.* 1380–1400, and finally the rebuilding of the central tower and much of the nave (work dated by inscriptions in wood and stone) following the collapse in 1520 of the earlier tower.

The church, 197 ft. (60m.) long (Fig. 8 and Plate 7), is mostly constructed of magnesian limestone and consists of an aisled chancel of five bays, transepts each of three bays, that to the N. having an E. chapel and that to the S. with an E. aisle, a central tower, and an aisled nave of six bays with a clerestory and a large S. porch. It retains a richly carved, moulded and painted sequence of roofs based on the camber-beam type, one signed by the carpenter W. Hall. Notable fittings are the early 15th-century stalls with 23 misericords, the painted chancel ceiling of 1445 with 40 panels depicting kings from Brutus to Henry VI, and the font of 1530. There are many 18th and 19th-century monuments and a chancel screen designed by Bilson. The church was restored in the 1850s by A. W. N. and E. W. Pugin and in 1864–7 by Sir Gilbert Scott.

St. Nicholas' Church (TA 04443943). The church is first referred to *c.* 1160 and probably arose as a chapel of ease to St. John's Minster in the early 12th century, although tradition ascribed its origins to St. John of Beverley.[3] Extensive rebuilding associated with the Holme family took place after 1346. It declined in use after the Reformation and the Civil War saw its end as a parish church, stone from it being used for fortifications. The parish was united with St. Mary's in 1667. Only the tower seems to have escaped demolition, but in 1693 some of its stones were used to repair the Minster and St. Mary's. In the 19th century, when the site was an osier-bed, many bones were unearthed, and in 1888 drainage work recovered squared and finely tooled stones. Excavations by Carr and MacMahon in 1938–9 exposed footings of a two-period chancel with N. aisle, N. and S. transepts, the former containing a chapel, an aisled nave and a W. tower (Fig. 9). Evidence of extensive 14th-century rebuilding was revealed. The whole structure was 120 ft. (36.6m.) long by 70 ft. (21.35m.) across the transepts.

St. Thomas's Chapel, of which little is known, is mentioned from 1366 onwards.[4] Leland recorded the tradition of a pre-Conquest foundation, at the time when the town was growing following Athelstan's grant of privileges. The Provost's Book compiled by Simon Russell in 1416–17 records that the chapel became more popular after the translation of St. Thomas Becket in 1220, because of its historical association with the saint, who was Provost of Beverley *c.* 1154 and also held the prebend of St. Michael, upon the lands of which the chapel was built.[5] MacMahon, commenting on this apparent confusion between the apostle and the martyred archbishop, suggests that the chapel may in fact have been founded in honour of the latter.[6] The Keepers' Accounts for 1450/51 place it near the Franciscan Friary, and an Elizabethan grant refers to 'St. Thomas Chapell close . . abutting on the east part on Queensgate', i.e. on the W. side of the street.[7]

RELIGIOUS HOUSES

Dominican Friary (TA 03883936). The Black Friars were already established at Beverley by 1240 when a provincial chapter of the order was held there.[8] A foundation before 1233 is suggested by the receipt in that year by Stephen Goldsmith, an ecclesiastic who provided land for the friary, of a pension for his services to the friars preachers. Thomas Holme gave a piece of ground 237 ft. long by 120 ft. broad for the erection of their house, and in 1263 they received a gift of 15 oaks from Henry III.[9] By 1310 the community numbered 42 and the 'long fourteenth and fifteenth century record of gifts and bequests from members of important Yorkshire families . . . as well as from humble Beverley burgesses, testifies to the high regard in which the friars were held'. The dormitory and library were accidentally burned in 1449 and a special donation towards rebuilding was made by the king. At its dissolution in 1539 the friary lay within a large area of orchards and gardens; some of its buildings were then put to secular use.[10] The Hull–Scarborough railway line was constructed across the site in 1846.

Rescue excavations undertaken by MacMahon in the early 1960s in advance of redevelopment revealed the W. foundations of the church and cloisters on the W. side of the railway.[11] The remainder of the claustral range and the central part of the two-phase church almost certainly lie beneath the railway line, but a significant portion of the church may well underlie gardens on the E. side of the track. Excavation revealed a number of burials within the buildings, some of which may have been among those listed in 1504 by John Wriothesley, Garter King at Arms.[12] The cemetery is mentioned in 1306 and the churchyard was one of the plots leased after the dissolution. Pottery recovered from the excavation was mostly 14th and 15th-century in date.

The surviving building on the site, probably the dormitory and library, (Plate 6) is a complex structure, largely of two phases.[13] The E. part has walls generally of chalk rubble, with some dressed limestone blocks. It stands on 14th-century footings of dressed stone with a continuous chamfered plinth.[14] The S. doorway, with its bold mouldings, is 14th-century; both this and the window surrounds are of dressed stone, as are the regularly spaced buttresses.[15] One of the much altered windows in the N. wall incorporates stone colonnettes, perhaps from the church or cloisters, and others can be seen in the first-floor windows of this part. Bases with circular sinkings for such colonettes can be seen in the section of the precinct wall W. of Eastgate. The two-storeyed brick porch on the S. is an addition, perhaps of the 16th century. The W. part of the building, built of brick, comprises a staircase flanked by a passage to the S. and by a small room on the N. Beyond this is a substantial ground-floor room below the Great Hall. From the early 19th century until the 1960s the building was divided into three separate dwellings, the Hall being subdivided into several rooms with a connecting passage.

The Great Hall retains its original simple hammer-beam roof truss; the beams flanking it were inserted to support the joists of a later ceiling. The main beam of the roof was given characteristic 15th-century moulding, but the joists (each numbered by the carpenter to correspond with the notches on the main beam) were quite plain. The original fire opening survives and externally a brick projection marks the site of a former chimney stack, shown on a drawing of *c.* 1758.[16] The brick internal partitions were plastered and painted with designs of varied character. Two murals in particular provide additional dating evidence. Within the porch is a pattern of large decorated circles separated by diamond interlace, white on black, corresponding with designs used on mid 16th-century embroidery.[17] In the N. reveal of the E. window is a polychrome pattern of birds, scrolls with 'Jhu mercy' and foliage (Fig. 10), probably representative of the scheme once covering the walls of the principal room in the W. wing.[18] Traces of it can also be seen on the subdivision between this room and the staircase under two layers of overpainting, one an ornate pattern of Elizabethan or Early Stuart character, the other Victorian work. A similar design in the recess over the staircase incorporates an as yet undeciphered black-letter inscription. A late 15th to early 16th-century date for this bird mural seems likely. This does not contradict MacMahon's suggestion that the building represents the dormitory and library rebuilt after the fire of 1449 (some of the stonework in the N. wall is reddened as if by fire), but Mackey regarded the

Fig. 10.   Dominican Friary: fragment of a late 15th to early 16th-century wall painting.

PLATE 6.   The Dominican Friary from the S., November 1979.

buildings as post-Reformation.

MacMahon's excavations revealed a vaulted drain which passed beneath the E. end of the building and, according to the O.S. 1:1056 map of 1854, extended N.W. as an open drain for 27m., probably connecting with the Hellgarth Lane 'Tan Dike'. Mackey excavated foundations 2 ft. (0.6m) below the 14th-century footings, belonging to an earlier building on the same alignment but of unrelated plan. This was in use in the early 13th century before being dismantled and buried by flood deposits. The site was then cultivated before the erection of the 14th-century building. Part of the area to the W. of the surviving building was also investigated by MacMahon, revealing several medieval and post-medieval walls stretching E. from Eastgate, associated with a well, drains, channels and hearths. The earliest medieval layers were not examined.[19]

The two gateways in the precinct wall of the Friary have moulded jambs and depressed Tudor arches. That now on the W. side of Eastgate also has a triangular pediment (Fig. 11); its former neighbour in Friars Lane had, until the 1960s, a multilobed gable of mid 17th–century character. Some limestone dressings are also incorporated in the frequently repaired precinct wall.

Franciscan Friary. The order is attested in Beverley by 1267; in 1297 a new friary was built 'without Keldgate Bar' on land given by William Lyketon and Henry Wygthon. Recent commentators have looked for the earlier site within the town boundary and have regarded High and Low Friars (TA 02973939), immediately beyond Newbegin Bar, as the second location. However, in an undated grant by Stephen de Crancewic which refers to St. Giles's Croft as lying S. of the Franciscan house, one of the witnesses was Hugh de Driffield, whose name also occurs in a charter of 1249–66.[20] If the same person was concerned in both documents, Crancewic's grant almost certainly predates 1297, indicating that High and Low Friars marks the first Franciscan site.

There, in the field behind Westwood and Albert Terraces, the foundations of several buildings were identified by some 19th-century antiquarians as belonging to St. Giles's Hospital.[21] Finds included foundations unearthed in 1843 at TA 02993942, a human skeleton, a stone coffin, an urn, a pavement and part of a column. The O.S. 1:1056 map of 1853 also indicates the site of a fishpond centred on TA 03053936, the course of a 'rampart' (TA 03053933–02903929–02893935), and the site of another rampart, probably a continuation of the first, along Albert Terrace.[22] In 1888 drainage excavations exposed old masonry at the base of a modern wall at the corner of Westwood Road (approx. TA 03013949) and, close to new houses adjoining Albert Terrace and near the Foundation School (now the Fire Station), the E. wall of, conjecturally, St. Giles's Chapel, fragments of the E. window and pieces of tessellated pavement (ap-

Fig. 11. Dominican Friary: 16th-century gateway in the precinct wall. This gateway and flanking sections of wall were moved in the 1960s from the E. to the W. side of Eastgate.

prox. TA 03023945). A stone coffin lay a few yards further N. and another was found in Mr. Kemp's garden in Westwood Road close to the burials already mentioned (approx. TA 02983948).[23] In the garden of 29 Westwood Road are a number of top sections of large stone mullions incorporating the springers for window tracery. In the early 1970s construction work revealed foundations at TA 03003943, near the site of the 1843 finds; unfortunately no record was made of these.[24]

The second friary 'without Keldgate Bar' was rebuilt in the 1350s and dissolved in 1539.[25] Entries in the Keepers' Accounts for 1450/51 indicate that the 'causeway' near the Greyfriars and the street near St. Thomas's Chapel (perhaps the present Queensgate) were either parts of the same street or two streets lying close together outside Keldgate Bar. When the Pilgrimage of Grace disturbances broke out in 1536, William Stapleton, one of the leaders, was staying at the Greyfriars, described as being very near to Westwood Green, and apparently only separated from it by a close and a hedge.[26] In about 1827 digging for clay in a field adjoining 'ffrer-lane' outside Keldgate Bar uncovered over 300 skeletons, extensive and thick stone foundations, and many artefacts including coins 'of the Richards and Edwards'. The lane ran near St. Martin's cemetery.

The land given for the second friary lay near St. Helen's Chapel,[27] the site of which should, therefore, have been near Keldgate Bar.

Carmelite Friary. Wills of 1376 and 1520 refer to four orders of friars at Beverley. Discounting confusion in the testators' minds (and other wills mention the four orders at Beverley and Hull), two more mendicant houses await discovery. The presence of the White Friars is further attested by another will of 1487, and Speed is said to refer to a house of Augustinians founded in

1287, apparently a confusion with the refoundation of the Franciscan house in 1297.[28]

Knights Hospitallers' Preceptory (TA 03853967). This was founded soon after 1201, when Sybil de Valloines gave to the order the manor of the Holy Trinity. On the eve of its dissolution in 1540 the Beverley preceptory was one of the wealthiest in England. The building still stood in Leland's time, and during the plagues of 1610 and 1664 it was superseded by, or utilised as, a pesthouse, which was still standing and kept in repair in 1750.[29] Both it and the rectangular moat which had surrounded the preceptory buildings are shown on Burrow's map of 1747 (Fig. 5.). The Inner Trinities was entered by an old gateway on the W. side a little to the N. of the 19th-century coal-depot offices behind Nos. 36–38 Trinity Lane. Although much of the site was obliterated by the construction of the railway station in the 1840s, the N. and E. sides of the moat were still visible in 1856, and the E. arm, eventually filled to make way for sidings, is shown on the O.S. 1:500 plan of 1892 as a wet ditch up to 5m. wide with a narrow channel linking its N. end to a drain running alongside Cherry Tree Lane.

The use of the ground as a garden in the early 19th century yielded several skeletons buried in separate graves, a stone coffin (now in the grounds of Beverley Public Library and Art Gallery), and many artefacts, including coins of the Tudor and Stuart periods. In 1825 many skeletons were uncovered at the N.W. angle of the Inner Trinities, some buried regularly but others thrown together indiscriminately in a large 'tumulus' (or 'tumuli'); these must represent the 17th-century plague victims. Recent excavations have disturbed further burials in the area between the railway and Cherry Tree Lane where 'Early English' stonework, bones and pieces of tessellated tile were found in 1888.[30]

HOSPITALS

St. Giles's Hospital (and Chapel). This, said by Leland to have been founded before the Conquest by Wulfe, is first recorded in the late 12th century. In 1277 it was annexed to Warter Priory and in 1279 Archbishop Wickwane ordained that there should be four priest brethren at the hospital which was to care for six sick priests and have fifteen beds for other sick folk. It was dissolved together with Warter in 1536 and its property granted to the Earl of Rutland. The site was probably in Lairgate between the street and the town ditch since a cemetery belonging to the hospital lay in Lairgate and St. Giles's Crofts lay to the W.[31] However Allen, Oliver and Poulson located it in the angle of Westwood Road and Albert Terrace, where foundations were discovered. These finds are now attributed to the Franciscan Friary and St. Giles's Crofts had an agricultural use; ridge and furrow is still visible in the school playing fields and in nearby gardens.

St. John's Hospital. The earliest reference to this hospital is in a will of 1444 and bequests were made to it from 1466 to 1475.[32] An Elizabethan grant mentions 'all that our tenement in Laregate . . . one orchard and one close . . . containing . . . one acre and a half of land now or late in the occupation of certain paupers called the Massendeu of St. John the evangelist . . . abutting on the east part on . . . Laregate'.[33] There were later two corporation almshouses in Lairgate, both on the W. side of the street, one of which may have arisen from the medieval foundation. The first, for men and known in the 19th century as Bede Houses, lay N.W. of the junction with Landress Lane (TA 03273948). A row of four late 18th to early 19th-century almshouses (Nos. 60–66) is built along the street frontage. The second, described in 1697 as 'one old Hospitall where severall poore women inhabit' lay in a close called Maisondieu Garth near the S. end of Lairgate.[34] The property was still known as Maisondieu at the end of the 19th century. The present buildings on the site date from the late 18th to early 19th century and are set back at right angles to the street (TA

03363914). Of the two this is perhaps the most likely successor to the medieval hospital. An enigmatic fragment of masonry is incorporated in an outbuilding there, namely, part of a limestone window jamb comparable in scale to the aisle windows of the Minster and far too large to have been part of a modest hospital building.[35] It may have come from the Minster or from one of the Greyfriars sites.

St. John the Baptist's Hospital. A garden in *Hayrerlane* held of this hospital is mentioned in a grant of 1440,[36] and an Elizabethan grant refers to 'all that tenement and one little garth there containing by estimation one rood of land commonly called St. John Baptist Massendeu now or late in the occupation of certain paupers abutting on the west part on a street called Fishmarket'. An adjoining property is described as 'abutting on the west part on . . . Eastgate'.[37] The site should therefore be sought on the E. side of Wednesday Market – Butcher Row and may have been succeeded by the former corporation almshouses described by Poulson as 'nine . . . rooms on the east side of Butcher-Row', as yet unlocated.[38] Alternatively it may be represented by one of the former church properties along this frontage (Map 2). Two lay on either side of Wilbert Lane (the medieval *Oswaldgate* or *Hayrerlane*)[39] and another, adjacent to Tyndall Lane in Wednesday Market, is now occupied by the Queen's Head.

St. Mary's Hospital (TA 029399). Bequests to this hospital were made from 1434 onwards, although a slightly earlier foundation can be deduced from the Keepers' Accounts for 1445 which, referring to rent from the land on which it stood, declared that such an arrangement had existed for twenty years.[40] In Leland's day it stood 'hard without the North *Bargate* of the Foundation of 2 Marchant Men, *Akeborow* and *Hogekin Overshal* . . . there is an Image of our Lady over this Hospitale Gate'.[41] The building was repaired in 1562. In 1792 the borough council investigated the buildings on the E. side of the North Bar and concluded 'that the maisondieu is in a ruinous condition and that the black-smith shop . . . is very old and in bad repair and . . . it would be advisable to take down such buildings and to erect two good dwelling houses thereon with footpath under the Bar'.[42] The 'maisondieu' is shown in an undated sketch (Plate 3) and may reasonably be identified as St. Mary's Hospital.[43]

St. Nicholas' Hospital (TA 03983936). First mentioned *c.* 1120,[44] this hospital was still standing, albeit in a decayed condition, in Leland's time near the Dominican Friary. It may have stood within the moated site, now destroyed, known as Paradise, from which or nearby came the remains of an ancient doorway, 'old curiosities' and foundations. Poulson, however, regarded the moated site as a place used by the Dominicans for contemplation.[45]

Trinity Hospital and Chapel (TA 03503953). This house was founded *c.* 1397 by John de Ake, a Beverley draper, on the *Crossbridge,* close to the junction of Toll Gavel and Walkergate.[46] It was built on an empty plot granted in 1394 by Thomas Frost to Robert de Garton and Henry Maupas, who were Ake's trustees. The plot, 120 ft. long and 80 ft. wide, abutted on the N. on the *Alta Via* and on the S. on the land of Thomas Danyll; its short sides were bounded on the W. by a tenement belonging to Danyll and on the E. by the 'common sewer de Walk-erbek'.[47] In 1399 tenements in the Cross Garths were used by the hospital. After its dissolution the stone-built chapel became the town's gaol. After a period of disuse the gaol was demolished in 1805 and its doorway was subsequently used as an entrance to warehouses at Beckside. Allen refers to an archway belonging to the site which served as a watercourse into Walkergate (i.e. Walkerbeck) drains.[48]

Other hospitals within the town are recorded in the 15th century. One, in Dead Lane, on the E.

side of St. Mary's churchyard, is mentioned in a will of 1475.[49] The other, mentioned in wills of 1475 and 1498, lay in Wood Lane.[50] Their sites may be indicated by the medieval church properties in these streets.

Leper-houses. Most larger medieval towns had at least one leper or lazar-house placed outside the defences, away from the built-up area. At Beverley one of two such establishments lay outside Keldgate Bar and is first referred to in a grant of 1332.[51] The site lay between *Cokewoldgate* and *Humbergate* (perhaps the present Cartwright Lane and Queensgate). Bequests were made to this house in 1399 and 1402, but shortly afterwards its site was leased by the Town Keepers.[52] Rent was paid in 1407 'for the leper house', in 1416 'for a common tenement . . . once the lepers house' and in 1450/51 for a certain empty place outside Keldgate Bar where the lepers once lived.[53]

The other building was outside the North Bar and seems to have replaced the earlier house. In 1402 a porch or lodge was added to an existing structure; a similar addition is mentioned in 1494.[54] Some 15th-century wills call this the *Spitelhouse,* and one of 1424 distinguishes between the 'poor lepers' and the 'poor' outside the North Bar; the latter were presumably the inmates of St. Mary's Hospital.[55] The Spittle House reappears in 18th-century Memorials in the Land Registry. In the 1770s the Rev. Robert Barker acquired a group of properties on the W. side of North Bar Without, comprising Spittle House Close . . two acres . . near to 'Spittle House' and Spittle House Garth, 55 yds. long and 27 yds. broad.[56] On Burrow's map of 1747 Barker's property is shown as stretching from North Bar Without to Hurn. The area (TA 02564003 – 02734015) is now occupied by Nos. 15–21 North Bar Without and by Hurn Lodge, Hurn Loft Cottage and Hurn Loft to the E.

OTHER BUILDINGS

The Guildhall. The site of the townsmen's 'han-shus' granted by Thurstan's charter is not known, but from 1282 the Keepers were using the hall in the Bishop Dings granted to the burgesses by Archbishop Wickwane in return for their surrender of rights in Beverley Parks. It was perhaps in this building, 'the Guild Hall, anciently called the Hanshouse' that the Magna Charta of the community was drawn up in 1359.[57] Rent for the Guildhall was paid in 1366 and 1386 to the Chapel of the Blessed Virgin Mary;[58] thereafter the Keepers rented the great hall of the merchant guild of St. John in Walkergate. The hall in the Dings, partly occupied by shops and provided with a bell for signalling the opening and closing of the market, was still used by the burgesses for business meetings. According to Witty, a new Common Hall, usually referred to in the town records as the *Gilda Aula*, rather than as the Hanshouse, was built at the S. end of the Dings in 1436. However, the Keepers continued to deal with borough affairs in the Walkergate hall until 1462 when they transferred to the hall in the Dings, taking over a part formerly leased to Robert Jackson, draper. The burgesses acquired a new Guildhall in 1501 with the purchase of Edward Minskip's 'great messuage' in the Cross Garths, and in 1502 £5 17s was spent in making 'a long chamber at the Crossgarths with the great part of the Hall'. The premises, which included 'a court or garthe', were served by a road giving access to Toll Gavel and perhaps also to Fish-marketmoorgate on the S.[59] This building was largely rebuilt in 1762–64, although its old front survived until 1832–33, when further substantial alterations were made, including the addition of a Doric portico. Although 19th-century writers stressed that the Tudor hall lay to the S. of the present Guildhall, on the site of the old gaol, its reconstruction on the same site is now thought more likely. The doorway of the old hall was re-erected in the 19th century by Gillyat Sumner at his Woodmansey residence (4 King Street), where it remains.[60]

Miscellaneous Finds. Several other finds indicate medieval buildings not discussed above. In the basement of 54 Keldgate, a late 17th-century house built for the Constable family, portions of 'stone walls of great antiquity' were formerly visible.[61] This house, which contains re-used 16th-century panelling, was refurbished in the 1770s for the grammar school master, whose 15th-century predecessor had also lived in Keldgate.[62] Excavations in 1858 across the S. side of Saturday Market Place came across an old drainage ditch, a thick brick pavement, part of a wooden post and several chisel-dressed stones which were thought to have formed the foundation of the pillory, removed from this site in 1688.[63] In 1812 a 'hedge fence' was found at a depth of 6 ft. (1.8m.) below Minster Moorgate,[64] and in 1888 sewerage excavations in an unspecified main street located a 'very good plank road' 6 or 7 feet below the surface.[65] Mains drainage excavations in Toll Gavel and Butcher Row in 1971 revealed road levels to a depth of 10 ft. (3m.) in places, with heavy timbers at this depth near the junction of Butcher Row and Walkergate. In 1979 excavations for a pipeline at the E. end of Grayburn Lane revealed fragments of moulded stone possibly dating from the 14th century.[66] In 1827 workmen digging the foundations of an old house belonging to H. Ellison in North Bar Within uncovered several human skeletons embedded in gravel some 7 ft. from the surface.[67] The collection of finds made by Dr. W. Stephenson and the extent of drainage operations and rebuilding suggest that more must have been discovered than was reported in the press or in local antiquarian literature.

Notes

1 Hearne 1774, IV, 102.
2 Bilson 1920. Other sources include Poulson, 723–64; Oliver, 345–65; Hope; Pevsner, 179–83; Hall and Hall, 27–33; MacMahon 1973, 29–30.
3 Carr and MacMahon; Poulson, 720–3, 732; Oliver, 49, 229, 272; *BI*, 11 Aug. 1888; Bulmer, 331; MacMahon 1973, 31, 58.

4 Poulson, 130, 724, 772; Oliver, 331.

5 Leach 1903, 335.

6 MacMahon 1973, 30–31.

7 BBR Town Keepers' Account Roll 1450/51, section on paving expenses; see also p. 30. The grant (BBR, Schedule 1–76; Poulson, App. 27) has been re-translated; see pp. 52–53 and notes 33, 37.

8 Palmer; Goldthorp, 387–95; *VCH*, 263–4; Poulson, 766–70; Oliver, 276; MacMahon 1973, 31–2; Hall and Hall, 34–6.

9 *Close Rolls, Henry III, 1261–1264*, 241.

10 A survey made *c.* 1539 of lands lying within the walls of the friary mentions a garden *(orti)* or orchard of 3 roods to the E. of the friary buildings; a pasture called Nesom garth, N. of the garden, of 1½ acres; a close called Eshe garth to the W. of Nesom garth, of ½ acre; a garden or orchard W. of this close, of 3 roods; a rood of garden called Ponde garth, and the churchyard, gardens and other little parcels to the S. and W. of the friary, containing 3 roods. PRO Special Collections, Rentals and Surveys, sc/Henry VIII/4571 m.9. See also Witty, *BG*, 30 Nov. 1929.

11 *Medieval Archaeology* 5 (1961), 314; 6–7 (1962–3), 317; 8 (1964), 245–6.

12 *Collectanea Topographica et Genealogica* IV (1837), 129–30; burials in the Franciscan Friary are also given on p. 129.

13 The description of the standing building is based on notes supplied by Dr. I. Hall.

14 Information from Mr. R. Mackey, 1978.

15 Similar window arch stones, probably of the 14th century, have been found during the recent excavations at Lurk Lane.

16 The drawing (British Museum 1971/10/11/9) is attributable to John Carr of York and shows his intended central tower for the Minster with a view of the W. end of the Friary building in the background.

17 See Hall and Hall, 35; their fig. 73 illustrates the mural behind the porch.

18 At the top and bottom of the reveal are black birds with wings and legs widely spread, above which are labels inscribed 'Jh(es)u Mercy'. An open-work rope of shaded green stems runs diagonally, each loop supporting sprays of trefoil with thistle-like purple flower heads, or of leaves, the whole interspersed with ermine tails. English and Neave, pl. 10, illustrate part of the mural from the alcove in the same room. Further areas of painting in the Great Hall can be seen behind the panelling in Hall and Hall, fig. 74, p. 35.

19 Unpublished; plans and notes are in Hull University Library archives (DDMM/2 SR 145–7).

20 Clay, 22.

21 Poulson, 778; Oliver 281, n.34; Goldthorp, 291–8.

22 The O.S. map also marks 'foundations discovered here' immediately S. of the rampart bounding High and Low Friars, in St. Giles's Crofts; these may belong to the friary or have some other, possibly post-medieval significance.

23 *BG*, 12 May, 21 April, 1888; *BI*, 14 April, 12 May, 20 May, 9 June, 1888.

24 Information from Dr. I. Hall, 1979. Large numbers of human bones have also been unearthed in the garden of No. 29.

25 Goldthorp, 292–8; *VCH*, 264–6; Poulson, 770–72; Oliver, 276; MacMahon 1973, 32; Brown 1906, 78; Leach 1900, 18; *Sketches*, 59; *BI*, 11 Aug. 1888.

26 Cox, 84. A post-dissolution survey of the friary made *c.* 1539 mentions a close of 2 acres called Esshe close adjoining Westwood Green and a highway leading to the green from the friary buildings. Other areas named are Cloyster garthes and Fraytor garth, both of one rood, and a close of one acre S. of the friary site called Butte close. PRO Special Collections, Rentals and Surveys, sc/Henry VIII/4571 m.8.

27 Allen, 180; Poulson, 770; Oliver, 120. 'Elena' is the usual spelling of the dedication.

28 Baker, 94; Raine 1868, 24; Raine 1884, 115; Allen, 180.

29 Allen, 181–2; Poulson, 779–83; Oliver, 193–4, 295–6; figs. 1–5; Sheahan and Whellan, 213, 226, 275–6; MacMahon 1973, 32; *VCH*, 261.

30 *BI*, 27 Oct. 1888. Witty mentions a road from 'the commandery' (the Inner Trinities) towards Cherry Tree Lane 'made of the same brick as that which may be seen in the wall bordering Grovehill Road near the railway crossing'–apparently referring to the former precinct wall of the Dominican Friary (*BG*, 5 July 1930).

31 Poulson, 775–9; Oliver, 268, 281; *VCH*, 301–2; Clay, 21–22. The rental of the Provostry in the 15th century mentions the house of the Master of St. Giles and 'a certain lane which runs from Minstermoorgate towards the church of St. Giles' (Leach 1903, 317).

32 *VCH*, 303–4; Raine 1855, 98.

33 BBR Schedule 1–76, p.2; Poulson, App. 37. Cf. n.7.

34 HCRO DDBC 16/27 and 16/30.

35 Information from Dr. I. Hall, 1979.

36 Hebditch, 24; *VCH*, 304.

37 Poulson, App. 36. Cf. n.7.

38 Poulson located the Crossgarths on the E. side of Butcher Row and mistakenly identified these almshouses as Ake's Trinity Hospital and Chapel (Poulson, 787 n. 2, 799 n. 3).

39 William Cotom's will of 1473 mentions 'the messuage in which he lives in the *alta via* de Fishmarketgate next to the common way of Oswaldgate otherwise called Hairelane' (B.I. Prob. Reg. IV, f. 199v).

40 In addition to a rent of 4*s.* 'from the poor people in the almshouse of the Gild of St. Mary near the North Bar and for a certain garden on the east side of the said house', the Town Keepers' Account Roll for 1450/51 records a rent of 14*s.* from 'the aldermen and stewards of the said Gild for the land on which the Maison Dieu is built within the North Bar'. This suggests that either the hospital extended onto land within the bar, or that there were two separate buildings on either side of the bar, both belonging to the same guild.

41 Leland I, 46; see also Poulson, 727; Oliver, 269; *VCH*, 303; HMC, 182.

42 BBR Beverley Borough Council Minute Books, 4 June and 2 July 1792; see MacMahon 1958, 76.

43 Witty remarks that 'several writers note having seen a statue of the Virgin over a hospital gateway at the North Bar' (*BG,* 16 Nov. 1929).

44 Smith, 194.

45 Poulson, 774–5, 791; Oliver, 276 n. 14; *BI,* 27 Oct. 1888; O.S. 1:1056 map (1854).

46 Poulson, 422, 730, 783–90, 799; Oliver, 302 n. 90; Clay, 26–33; *VCH,* 303–4.

47 BBR Schedule III/2.

48 Allen, 190. The Town Keepers' Account Roll for 1502/3 includes rents for nine tenements at *lez Crosgarthes,* one called *yatehowse,* and three gardens, once called *le pownde garth.*

49 *VCH,* 304; MacMahon 1973, 33.

50 *VCH,* 304; Raine 1868, 133.

51 Poulson, 773; Oliver, 269; *VCH,* 304; BBR Schedule III/2.

52 B.I. Prob. Reg. III, f. 24 and ff. 71v–72.

53 See Town Keepers' Account Rolls (BBR) and HMC, 123, 131, and 159.

54 Poulson, 222, 773–4; Leach 1900, 42.

55 B.I. Prob. Reg. III, f. 205v.

56 HCRO Registry of Deeds G44/94; H194/405; I313/652; I388/853; also I386/848.

57 HMC, 14–15.

58 BBR Town Keepers' Account Rolls, 1366, 1386; see HMC, 156–7.

59 Poulson, 422; Oliver, 294 n. 66; Sheahan and Whellan, 283–4; HMC, 14, 54, 141, 156–7, 159; Witty, *BG,* 31 May 1930; MacMahon 1973, 49–50. A grant of 1417 describes the Minskip property as 'a capital messuage and orchard with free entry to the *Alta Via* (i.e. Toll Gavel) on the north and east, and to Fishmarketmoregate on the south' (BBR Schedule III/13.9a). A grant of 1433 refers to the lower gates (*portas inferiores*) on the E. side of the property (ibid.,16B). The 'lane by Gildhaule' is mentioned in a list of streets cleaned in 1502, and a *volte* or enclosed sewer there was repaired in the same year (BBR KA 1502). BBR Schedule III/13 contains the deeds relating to the Minskip messuage and Guildhall site from 1320 to 1501. For the earlier archbishops' hall, see Poulson 78, 79, 185; Farrer 137; MacMahon 1973, 18. Repairs in Aug. 1981 revealed a complete timber-framed wall with a central doorway at the E. end of the Guildhall courtroom.

60 English and Neave, 6 and pl. 11.

61 YASRS 27 (1899), xlix.

62 Leach 1898, 95.

63 Oliver, 291–2; *BG,* 21 Aug. 1858; Bulmer, 329; Dennett, 178.

64 Oliver, 26, 298.

65 *BG,* 27 Oct. 1888.

66 Information from Mr. G. P. Brown, Beverley Local History Library.

67 Oliver, 298.

PLATE 7.   North Bar Within, painted by George Barrett c. 1776/7. From the original at Burton Constable Hall.

POST-MEDIEVAL BUILDINGS

DATING

The annexed map of the former municipal borough (Map 2) shows five basic building periods, but because the periods chosen are not quite the conventional ones the choice requires explanation. They were selected to show those major shifts in emphasis directly related to the building history of Beverley, though they also reflect similar changes in the architectural development of both Hull and York, for the local style was influenced by both these major centres and, like them but unlike so many county towns, Beverley had its own important group of town houses occupied by the gentry during the Season.

It has nevertheless been difficult to select any grouping of dates which accurately reflect the complex architecture of the borough. Periods based upon national stylistic changes only make sense where enough extant buildings of each principal period survive to warrant such a linkage, but at best such broad treatment necessarily ignores the many possible local variations. Thus in Beverley the great churches alone represent the major Gothic styles, with but modest support from domestic and civic buildings. Similarly there is too little of Tudor or Stuart date to warrant further separate categories. On the other hand the terse descriptions 'Georgian' or 'Victorian' would conceal too many of those variations that add so much to the character of Beverley. The classification of buildings by century or half century or by the reigns of successive monarchs is equally unsatisfactory, and so an attempt is here made to devise a sequence of periods to help those who wish to study the town's buildings for themselves.

To 1690. No attempt has been made to portray the building sequence of the Minster, of St. Mary's, or of the demolished churches and friaries. Except for the North Bar, the remaining medieval secular structures are of such simple and fragmentary character that precise dating is as yet difficult, but nothing would seem to survive from before 1400. Equally difficult to discover is just when the town's house builders changed over from timber to brick. (No evidence has come to light of domestic buildings constructed in stone). Brick clay was locally abundant, and ample chalk was easily accessible from which to make a tolerable mortar and to use for other building purposes. The decline of the house-carpenter and the rise of the bricklayer may well have taken a century, but by the last third of the 17th century brick seems to have been used for all but the humblest dwellings, even in the nearby rural areas. The handful of buildings surviving from this period of transition is included for convenience with those of the earlier period, though they too were the work of craftsmen as yet not too aware of the latest London fashions.[1]

1690–1740. The second phase was markedly different, for Beverley then enjoyed a surge of prosperity, represented by the first flowering of a consistently classical manner. The London architects Nicholas Hawksmoor (1664–1736), Colen Campbell (1676–1729) and, not far away, Sir John Vanbrugh (1664–1726) and Lord Burlington (1694–1753) were also employed. Their high standards gave the greatest encouragement to local craftsmen, though the architect's control was not then such as to crush the individuality of the more ambitious craftsman here, notably the carver-architect William Thornton of York (1675–

1721) or the Issott family of master masons. Both were among the leading craftsmen employed upon the important restoration of Beverley Minster between 1716 and the 1730s.[2] The scale of operations was such that it involved nearly 400 other craftsmen, a number that reveals the real prosperity of the contemporary building industry in the town. Moreover, Beverley men found employment in the building and furnishing of several of the local great country houses, notably Burton Constable.[3] The style they evolved was in the mainstream of East Yorkshire vernacular but with an admixture of London and Continental motifs.

1740–1780. The succeeding period may be typified by the overlay of pattern-book motifs, especially for internal and external doorcases and internal fittings, such as chimneypieces, stucco ceilings and staircase balustrades. The main outer doorcase of 51 Keldgate, derived from plate XXVII of Batty Langley's *Builder's and Workman's Treasury of Designs* dated 1739, may be cited and the chimney piece in the Music Room is an adaption of plates 52–53 of William Kent's *Designs of Inigo Jones,* Vol. 2, 1727. Some of the decoration of Norwood House can be traced to similar sources. As yet all this decoration was hand-wrought and of natural materials, but the rapid growth in both local and national prosperity created such demands on the building industry, especially from the craftsmen involved in decorative work, that great efforts were made to speed up the manufacture of ornament. Papier mâché (found at Norwood House) was among the first in the field but was unsuitable for exterior work. Then came 'Composition', Coade stone, cast plaster and cast or stamped metals, all but cast plaster being usable indoors or out. During the 1760s and 1770s such materials were often used in the most fashionable of English houses; thereafter demand spread to the smaller towns and those villages nearer the main centres of population.

1780–1860. The import of mass-produced and sometimes synthetic products inevitably meant the dilution of local style, because the new motifs were designed elsewhere and were often demonstrably inspired from fashionable London sources. Thus, distinct from earlier practice, there was no modification of motifs to accord with local preference, for the urn or the garland were the same wherever they were sold. The matter is complicated by the fact that greater prosperity and the ever-reducing cost of applied decoration meant that it was easy to modernise, perhaps with a new outside doorcase or a set of new chimneypieces for the principal rooms. This outcome of the Industrial Revolution was hastened by the spread firstly of the canal network and then by that of the earlier railways. Both were to make the bringing to Beverley of hitherto very expensive raw materials more economic, for example, of good building stone for the splendid porticoes on the Sessions House (*c.* 1804–14) and on the Guildhall (1832). For those who could not afford stone stucco was a socially acceptable substitute, for in its earlier days of use it was 'frescoed' to simulate the veinings of natural stone.

1860–1914. The final period represents the era when local style gave place to one more regional in character; not unnaturally the Beverley style almost merged with that of Hull. Both towns were loth to give up the classical for the revived gothic, though Hull architects such as R. G. Smith and F. S. Brodrick unhesitatingly introduced the latter style among the Georgian and Regency houses of North Bar Without. They were aided by the brilliant woodcarver James Edward Elwell (1836–1926) and his equally competent studio employees. Nonetheless Beverley retained a noticeable cultural independence from its larger neighbour, and architects such as William Hawe (1822–97) had a wide practice in the vicinity, usually working in a classical style overlaid by Georgian and continental motifs, much as his 18th-century predecessors had done. A characteristic Hull motif was the use of glazed patterned tiles as a dado within entrance porches.[4] This final period thus held a contrast between the idiosyncratic artist-craftsmanship of men such as Elwell and the ubiquitous decorative elements brought in by rail from all over the British Isles.

CHURCH HOUSE PROPERTY

Church-ownership has always played a significant part in the town's building history, though the holding has varied greatly. It probably reached its peak by the 15th or earlier 16th century but then, at the Reformation, suffered so catastrophic a decline that neither the Minster nor the other surviving parish church, St. Mary's, had either a capital investment or rents equal to the needs of the church fabrics. In 1579 the Crown restored at least some of the properties confiscated at the Reformation, though there is no reason to believe that it granted properties other than those once held by the Church.[5] This nucleus was modestly extended by gift and purchase. The more substantial properties were kept in repair and from time to time improved in collaboration with the tenants, but the Church proved equally ready to allow redevelopment by a lessee if its income would show a worthwhile eventual gain. Most of the surviving medieval houses in the town are, or were until comparatively recently, church properties. There was, however, significant redevelopment in the Georgian period creating Newbegin Bar House and 35 North Bar Within, both newly built by Thomas Wrightson,[6] and the terrace houses on the S. side of Minster Moorgate.[7] In the 19th century redevelopment was spasmodic. No. 37 North Bar Within was a bold semi-detached pair of houses designed by Cuthbert Brodrick in 1861, and a series of houses at the S. end of Highgate was new-built. The properties marked on Map 2 are those defined in the Minster property book of 1867[8] and the St. Mary's property book of 1837.[9]

BUILDING MATERIALS

Stone
The Beverley area is not blessed with first-class building materials and so, when their use seemed desirable, they had to be brought here at considerable expense. The Trent, the Ouse and their tributaries, the Humber and the Hull were the principal routes, with, from the Hull, the canalised Beck linked to the town centre via Flemingate. Good building stone is absent, though chalk was dug on the Westwood and used chiefly to raise the level of low-lying ground, to serve as foundation material, or as infill between skins of brick or stone. Thick layers of rough chalk blocks were uncovered on sites near Sow Hill Road in 1979, and similar blocks were seen used as foundation material for the wall of 19–21 Ladygate. As a walling material chalk can be seen at the Minster and the Dominican Friary. A better building stone was quarried near North and South Cave, an oolitic limestone brownish in colour and of a fairly coarse texture. This was used in the Minster before 1213, after which magnesian limestone from the Tadcaster area was used, a stone which also occurs, in re-used fragments, on the Dominican Friary site and in excavated fragments on the Greyfriars site S. of Westwood Road. Most of St. Mary's church is also constructed from this stone.

No firm evidence exists for the use of stone for domestic or civic work during the medieval, Georgian or Victorian periods, other than for minor details such as window sills, plinths, string courses, kneelers, quoins, cornices, doorways and porticoes, though notable exceptions are the Sessions House and the front of the Guildhall. The former St. Mary's Manor (Plate 7) may have had a stone façade, and Hotham House, Eastgate (*c.* 1713–21), is known to have been of brick with dressings of Roche Abbey stone, from a famous quarry on the Yorkshire–Nottingham border. The high cost of using stone is illustrated by the use during the early Georgian restoration of the Minster of demolition material from St. Mary's Abbey, York, but the growth first of the canal network and then of the railways reduced the cost of transport sufficiently to encourage moderate use of stone during the 19th century. The black 'touch' used for the more expensive grave-stones and for the chequers in the paving of Georgian floors is probably black marble imported from Holland or Belgium. Only two examples of Coade's artificial stone have been discovered locally in use as a building material, namely, a keystone and paterae dated 1790 formerly at 31 Butcher Row and the statue of Justice of 1809 on the Sessions House.[10]

Timber.
The comparative scarcity of good building stone was paralleled by that of good building timber, for the oak favoured by medieval builders was not locally abundant. Hence it was used more sparingly than in comparable structures in or W. of the Pennines. Oak for use at the Minster was brought from the Forest of Galtres near York by order of the arch-bishop, but how much oak was used elsewhere in the town, whether native or imported, has not so far been determined. In the 1540s Leland described Beverley as 'large and welle buildid of wood',[11] and timber framing was undoubtedly the standard constructional system used in the locality until perhaps the close of the 16th century. Thereafter the house carpenter faced increasing competition from the bricklayer until, by the end of the 17th century, the latter had prevailed in both town and country. Cruck frames were certainly used in rural areas, but none has been recorded within the town itself. In style Beverley timber framing was characteristic of that of Eastern England, with thin, closely spaced studs, occasional strengthening with curved braces, and jetties supported by a sequence of bold brackets, as at 49 North Bar Within (Plate 8). The carving, moulding and decorative panelling so popular in Western England are absent, so are the ranges of gables, projecting oriel windows or the picturesque overhanging of floor by floor to be found elsewhere.

Only those timber-framed houses now exist which were capable of adaptation or were of generous size. No single-storied examples remain, even if there were possibly once many such. In addition to natural decay and demolition the added problem arose of the repeated raising of the street levels with the effect of curtailing the height of ground-floor rooms. Only 4–6 Highgate (demolished in the 1950s without either adequate record or salvage of significant detail) broke the rule of simplicity with its carved tracery window heads and a carved and moulded bressumer or cornice between the ground floor and the jettied first floor. This 15th-century house was not unique; others such as the adjacent Englebert Hall or Daunt's House in Toll Gavel were properties of substantial size, but their appearance has not been recorded.[12] The Highgate house and all other survivors had an infill of brick, as was normal in York, not wattle and daub. Plain coursed brickwork seems general, but the Sun Inn in Flemingate has panels of good herring-bone infill, and

PLATE 8.   No. 49 North Bar Within, November 1979.

the Friary, 11 Ladygate and houses elsewhere have thinner infill panels of brick or tile on edge, plastered over on both sides to give a total wall thickness of 3–4 in.[13]

Not enough research has been done on domestic timber roofs for a pattern sequence to emerge, but excellent work survives at 19–21 Ladygate, 31–33 Saturday Market, the S. wing of 25 Highgate (the Monk's Walk, formerly the George and Dragon), and at the Friary. On a much grander scale there are the roofs of the Minster and of St. Mary's church. Timber ridge pieces are generally absent. Floors often have one or more deep supporting beams to subdivide the area into more manageable units, a practice which enabled the sizes of joists to be reduced. The latter are sometimes housed in notches cut into the transverse beam, sometimes they simply rest on it.

The counterparts of these beams in the 16th and 17th centuries had a simple quarter-round moulding cut into the lower angles, as at 34–36 North Bar Within or 44 Market Place. Most medieval floor joists, which were of rectangular cross-section, were laid flat with their longer side parallel to the floor; the later examples were at right angles to the floor. By the late 17th century the exposed underside of timber floors was unfashionable and many were ceiled over. One such, in Market Place, Hull, had decorative paintings covering the joists, but in Beverley only a red-ochre colour has been found (at 25 Highgate), though there are claims that 'Tudor' painted work was found years ago at 11 Wednesday Market. Exposed floors were still erected in smaller houses during the 18th century, such as are visible at 7 Walkergate and 4 Ladygate.

The usual steep pitch of earlier roofs indicates the once prevalent use of thatch, an indication confirmed by the descriptions given in the older leases of church properties which reveal that some houses had fashionable flat tiles at the front, pantiles at the side and thatch at the back.[14] Church leases sometimes also refer to 'Blue Dutch tiles' or to 'Holland tyles',[15] but how these differed from the native product is not clear; perhaps they were glazed, like those to be seen at Burton Constable.

The majority of timber-framed houses are now largely concealed behind 18th or 19th-century brick or stucco, e.g. 7–9 North Bar Within, 19–21 or 35 Ladygate (Plate 12), and 16–24 Hengate. At 1 Highgate the joist ends of the former jettying alone remained visible until they were recently plastered over. Sometimes a fragment of jettying is indicative of an early date, as at 54 Market Place where examination of the interior confirms such dating. Sometimes old timber framework is exposed during alterations, to be later re-covered as at 34–36 North Bar Within or at 9 and 23 in the same street where it was left open to view. At 7 Wednesday Market the vertical timbers had long since decayed and

PLATE 9.   No. 15 Flemingate, November 1979.

been replaced by a quickly made infilling of broken tiles and mortar.

During the last quarter of the 17th century many builders crowned their houses with heavy classical cornices, typified by the fragment at 7–9 Butcher Row and by the handsome example at 14–16 Newbegin. As an alternative some houses were constructed with a cove of lath and plaster between the wooden elements, as at 48 North Bar Without (apparently late 17th-century, much repaired and altered *c.* 1730).[16] Subsequent decay has resulted in the disappearance of many similar wooden cornices, the site of which is often marked by a plain fascia-board punctuated by projecting wooden gutter brackets, as at 65 Toll Gavel (*c.* 1703) or 62 North Bar Without (*c.* 1732). Mid-Georgian wooden cornices were of more modest dimensions; good examples are 17 Highgate with its unusual guttae beneath the modillions, 1 Saturday Market built by William Middleton with standard modillions, and 6–8 Newbegin which has the more elegant dentils typical of the neo-classical style. In the early 18th century the doorcase was often no more than a lengthened window opening, as at 3–4 North Bar Within and formerly at 43–44 Market Place, but from the 1730s until the 1860s the classical doorcase became standard, though with very varied detail. Good pattern-book examples may be seen at 48 and 56 North Bar Without, Bar Chambers and 55–56 North Bar Within, 37 Saturday Market and, of later date, on both sides of Railway Street. The carved oak Roman Doric doorcase towards the garden at 10 Newbegin is, however, a remnant of the former nave galleries at the Minster removed in 1826.

Brick

Much the most obvious building material in Beverley is brick. The history of its use in the town is complex because it has been regularly used here since at least the 14th century. The abundant local deposits of brick clay produce bricks of a reddish-brown colour, whereas from further afield, near the Humber banks, deposits of gault clay yield a creamy-white brick popular from *c.* 1780 until the close of the 19th century. Possibly some bricks at least were imported into the district from Flanders as ballast, and bricks with a greenish-brown hue found at the Friary are indeed similar in colour to those from the Low Countries. The precise source of stock bricks, finely textured, kiln-burnt, and of good, red, even colour has not been established, but they were used for principal façades and for arches over windows and doors. Their manufacture and transport may have formed part of the Humber trade and merits further investigation.

The vault over the Minster nave, the North Bar of 1409 and work at the Dominican Friary (in part restoration work said to have followed the fire of 1449) are examples of medieval brickwork. The two later gateways in the Friary precinct wall are also of brick and one formerly had a Dutch gable of mid 17th-century character.

Little evidence of building activity in Beverley survives from between the Reformation and the Civil War, even church monuments are few, but thereafter the tempo quickened as town merchants and county gentry alike began to vie with each other in building, scanning the pattern books of their day for new ideas in decoration, often enough of continental inspiration. The first phase in this revival coincided with a liking for 'Artisan Mannerism', a style characteristic of the Low Countries which first gained a firm hold in S.E. England just before the Civil War. In Beverley the style is well represented by 58 Flemingate and in the N. wing of the courtyard of 25 Highgate where, in work dated 1671, giant Doric pilasters frame former window openings crowned by triangular and segmental pediments. The style, if not necessarily consistency of material, was continued

PLATE 10.   Walkergate, the N. end, looking N., *c.* 1900.

at the former St. Mary's Manor, where Doric pilasters recall contemporary Yorkshire country houses, such as Cowick and Nun Monkton, rather than standard town houses of the locality.

The succeeding generation, building from the 1680s onward, put greater reliance on fine brickwork and good proportion, with bold, moulded brick or timber cornices, bolection-moulded doorcases, as at 14–16 Newbegin, and symmetrical repetition of tall, rectangular window openings fitted with oak mullions and transoms and glazed with leaded lights. English bond was retained for the backs and sides of buildings, but the front was more often in Flemish bond, i.e. with alternating headers and stretchers in each course. Touches of conservatism, however, occurred, notably twinned gables at the back of a roof fashionably hipped at the front; examples survive at 14–16 Newbegin, 7 Hengate and 7–9 Butcher Row. Bricks were a little shorter than earlier, 9 ins. or so instead of 10 ins., 4 ins. wide and about 2 ins. deep. These measurements contrasted with the attempted standardisation by statute to give a size of 9 by 4½ by 3 ins. From the mid 18th century to the 1830s the thickness of bricks was more often 2¾ ins.; the regulation size was not common in Beverley until the 1840s. Why the disparity in sizes lasted for so long is uncertain, so is the reason for eventual compliance. Aesthetically, small bricks can enhance the scale of smaller buildings, though more must be laid over a given area.

The finest brickwork had thin joints of pure white lime putty and great care was taken to line up the vertical as well as the horizontal joints, a point of particular importance with the strong pattern of Flemish bond. Neat jointing was also needed for the moulded cornices in vogue from *c.* 1680 to 1780. Some such were of conventional classical profile, as at 15 Highgate, Tymperon's Hospital in Walkergate, or at 19 Toll Gavel; others had bold modillions, as at 54 Keldgate or 119 Walkergate, or, still more refined, had small dentils as at 51–53 Toll Gavel or 55–63 North Bar Within, their very delicacy revealing a late date. Even the earliest type of cornice, found on the North Bar itself, survived in use until the later 18th century (as can be seen at 31–33 Keldgate) as an alternative to the cornice much more frequently found on smaller houses and cottages all over England, with a row of alternately projecting headers between the oversailing courses. There are good examples of the latter in the terraced houses on the S. side of Minster Moorgate and at 6 Ladygate.[17] The speculative developer Dr. Nicholas Barbon (*c.* 1640–1698) claimed that he could tell at a glance the trade of the master-builder responsible for each house.[18] Hence in Beverley it is known that many of the houses with brick cornices were built by William and Thomas Wrightson, whose activities included that of brickmaker, whereas William Middleton (1730–1815), a joiner, built houses with wooden cornices. Stonemasons such as the Rushworths liked to include in their houses at least a stringcourse of stone.[19]

Much the best examples of brick vaulting of post-medieval date are those at 'Arden's Vaults' next to 16 Hengate and the series beneath the former Tiger Inn at 43–47 North Bar Within of *c.* 1730. No. 15 Highgate is in effect built upon an elliptically-arched bridge, presumably because of the high water table.

The cheapest (and weakest) brickwork was built of clamp-burnt brick in garden-wall bond, where between every header course are two or more courses of stretchers. It was certainly in use by the end of the 17th century, e.g. for the perimeter wall of the St. Mary's Manor site. The external appearance of headers in English or Flemish bond is no guarantee that they bind the inner and outer skins of a wall, for in practice through bonding was difficult to achieve where stock bricks of uniform size were backed by coarser clamp-burnt bricks. Hence through bonding was spasmodic and the walls' strength was consequently reduced. To make matters worse, the vogue for window seats tempted builders to provide only 4½ ins. thickness of wall beneath a window sill.

During the last quarter of the 18th century builders began to exploit the local seams of gault clay. At a distance, and when new, gault bricks might be mistaken for stone, as at the Sessions House; they also harmonised with stucco until darkened by deposits of soot, when they contrasted with painted stucco. The dual use of gault bricks for the wings and painted stucco for the remainder is shown at 11 Cross Street built *c.* 1834.[20] The usual thickness of earlier gault brick was 2¾ ins. Stone-coloured brick and stucco tempted others to paint their existing red brick walls in stone colour, or at least to paint their brick cornices and window heads thus, a fashion that paradoxically led to builders supplying window heads which were thin stone slabs incised with false joints simulating those of brick as a cheaper alternative to building up a window arch out of expensive rubbed or gauged brick, a deception masked by paint. Dummy joints also appeared, cut into the surface of the specially shaped, long, arch bricks popular during the late 18th and 19th centuries. The incisions were pointed up to match the rest. Moulded fireclay too, once painted, also deceived the eye.

As well as serving as a crowning feature the earlier brick cornices had the functional purpose of helping to throw rainwater clear of the walls, but by the close of the 18th century this sluicing of rainwater from roofs was no longer acceptable, and the provision of wooden gutters and downspouts of wood, lead, or later iron, was ordered. The nuisance was eventually abated, though not without aesthetic loss, for the guttering puts much fine brickwork into shadow.

Victorian brickwork in Beverley followed Georgian precedents. There are fine window arches at the Railway Station, and Cuthbert Brodrick (1821–1906) used moulded brick arches at 37 North Bar Within, but strongly polychromatic brickwork was avoided, nor was much use made of those strips or panels of decorative motifs commonplace elsewhere.

BUILDING TYPES

Of the four main categories of building, church, civic, domestic and commercial, church building suffered an obvious decline after the Reformation. The friaries were quickly pillaged for their materials, St. Martin's chapel was demolished as redundant and St. Nicholas' church became ruinous. For the Minster and St. Mary's there were the twin problems of maintenance and the need to accommodate a steadily rising population. No 17th or 18th-century chapels now survive; the oldest Nonconformist chapel is that of *c.* 1808 off Dyer Lane, a simple brick-built room without architectural pretension.

Civic work was more impressive. The late medieval Guildhall was remodelled and extended in the 1760s and refronted in 1832 at the Corporation's expense.[21] The financing of the construction of the Market Cross involved both the Corporation and the town's two members of Parliament; work dragged on from 1708 to 1715.[22] The next two significant Corporation schemes were the building in 1753–4 of the Corn Exchange[23] and of a new Fish Market in 1777,[24] both of brick with stone dressings and now both demolished. They lay to the E. of the Dings, a row of houses gradually rebuilt to a similar pattern from 1740 to 1758.[25] Exact uniformity was not demanded; newer buildings took their neighbours as models.

Bold town planning ventures gained no worthwhile adherents, for even those as modest as the Regency scheme for Cross Street[26] or the slightly later Railway Street,[27] remained incomplete. For the rest it was a case of the gradual rebuilding of existing premises, often enough with the amalgamation of the sites of run-down medieval properties and the substitution of one building, or perhaps a pair or a short terrace, of more substantial character. Sometimes the process of site accumulation took place over a prolonged period. The present 7 Hengate (built 1708–09)[28] is on the site of eleven, perhaps twelve, houses and a stable, the boundary not being rounded off with its garden until 1930. The typical medieval frontage could have as modest a width as 9½–11 ft., as at 9 and 11 Ladygate, 3 Saturday Market or 13 Butcher Row, widths presumably related to the convenient span of the beams that carried the first floor. Hence many later houses are multiples of their medieval predecessors. The materials of the latter were usually carefully salvaged for re-use as floor joists or roof timbers, or as walling where appearance was of no great consequence.[29] Site amalgamations can often be traced through the Memorials in the former East Riding Land Registry. Unfortunately before the 19th century plans of property are the exception in this source and generally.

Sometimes, where garden space on one side of a road was expensive, the wealthier house owners bought up the houses opposite to incorporate their sites into a new garden. Houses were acquired for this purpose opposite the Hotham House in Eastgate from 1713 onwards, but the demolition of the latter in 1766 was not followed by a full building on

PLATE 11.   Nos. 33–9 Butcher Row, pre-1912.

the site of the garden created opposite on the W. side of the street.[30] A similar process made up the garden of 14–16 Newbegin on both sides of that street,[31] and church-owned houses fronting North Bar Within (Plate 7) were demolished to enhance the garden of St. Mary's Manor, and again not replaced.[32] Less often adopted elsewhere was the practice of allowing individual owners to raise the causeway outside their houses at their own expense.[33] Such houses usually faced the sun and so tended to be rebuilt more often than their sunless neighbours opposite. The raising of the causeway and of the roadway disadvantaged the older properties; those which were too low once the roadway had been raised were reduced in value, some were converted to other uses and others remodelled to give them a further lease of life. Thus Hengate and Newbegin have tall houses on one side fronting pavements and lower houses on the other devoid of pavements.

Where gardens have replaced houses the sites could prove to be of archaeological interest. On the other hand, old gardens were occasionally built over, provided access was available from the street. The frontage house with courtyard houses behind it was a frequent medieval development, but Beverley maps and documents point to courtyard housing of post-medieval date, though not precluding similar earlier arrangements. The majority have been destroyed during slum clearance, but a few still exist as offices behind 38 North Bar Within and parts of former front walls can be seen in Tindall Lane off Wednesday Market. Where access to back land proved awkward, the latter has remained undeveloped, as in the areas bounded by Keldgate, Minster Moorgate, Lairgate and St. John Street, behind the frontages of Highgate, and within the area from Hengate to Wylies Road and from Manor Road to North Bar Within. Suburban ribbon development of the frontages occurred in North Bar Without, where a few former farm-houses have been drastically remodelled to suit urban tastes.

The old mixture of domestic, commercial and industrial use in buildings is less easy to disentangle, for commonly until well into the 19th century a single property could fulfil all these functions. During building booms many commercial, industrial and stable buildings were either demolished to make way for new houses or were adapted to serve as domestic premises. Shop fronts too were inserted into houses, a change which during the 18th century prompted the Corporation to charge a small sum as compensation for obstruction to the pavement.[34] The oldest surviving shop front is at 28 Saturday Market; later ones can be seen at 27 and 32–34 Saturday Market, in Norwood, Eastgate and Wood Lane. The steadily falling cost of plate glass revolutionised the design of shop fronts; early use of large panes can be seen at 11 Saturday Market and 99–100 Walkergate. The shutters are still closed nightly at 28 Saturday Market and were, until recently, at No. 27. Shop-keepers expected to live over their shops and their principal living rooms were typically on the first floor, but the practice of having a first-floor sitting or drawing room is still commonplace elsewhere in the town.

The numerous reference to 'mills' in property deeds almost always were to horse-mills; like the equally numerous tanneries these have seemingly disappeared without trace. The earlier wholly industrial buildings tended to be in the E. half of the town; examples are the warehouses at or near Beckside and Flemingate, the early tannery premises in Flemingate and Keldgate, and the various ironworks near the railway station. A few of these buildings may date from the latter half of the 18th century. The Gas Works of 1824 was sensibly sited near the coal wharves; its imposing gateway still survives. Breweries were closer to the centre; one important one was behind Toll Gavel, another was in Ladygate. Despite a promising start, however, Beverley failed to develop as an industrial town.

Buildings designed for public entertainment included the Assembly Rooms of 1761–63 in Norwood, extended in 1838 and replaced by a cinema,[35] and a succession of small theatres. The shell of the theatre built c. 1754 survives at 90–92 Walkergate,[36] as do fragments of the theatre of c. 1802 in Lairgate,[37] but no traces appear to survive of those built behind Toll Gavel and in Wood Lane.

DETAILS

Technical innovation in design or construction is absent before the first half of the 19th century, though two examples of laminated-wood construction may be noted: the tentative experiment in lamination in the early Georgian roof of the N. transept of the Minster and the fully developed roofing system of the Salvation Army Citadel of 1885 in Wilbert Lane.[38] For the rest, conventional materials and methods went unchallenged.

These conventional methods inevitably shaped the architectural style in the locality and, as in Hull, master-builders contrasted external simplicity with internal display, giving a richness now best seen in staircases and panelling where they survive. Unfortunately they have steadily diminished in numbers in the last twenty years as shop owners 'modernise' their premises. In many cases the size of a building is not a good indicator of the quality of its internal fittings. Thus there is a handsome, if diminutive, late 17th-century staircase at 13 Butcher Row with balusters equal to those in much grander contemporary stairs, such as at 65 Toll Gavel or in the secondary staircases at 54 Keldgate or 14–16 Newbegin, and finely carved and turned balustrades survive at 11 Saturday Market and 19 North Bar Within.

The typical frontage of *c.* 1680–1760 laid stress on the horizontals, namely, a hipped roof, a bold cornice and rows of windows, typified by the handsome front of 14–16 Newbegin or by 48 North Bar Without. If full symmetry was not possible without internal inconvenience, the door could be placed off-centre in four-bay fronts, as at 26 Norwood or 7 Hengate. The former is of *c.* 1714,[39] but its later Victorian neighbour, No. 28, is of similar composition, though with a change in roof pitch and in the proportions of its windows. The impact of window tax (imposed in 1696 and abolished in 1851) did, however, tempt many builders and householders to reduce the number of their windows, as is evident at 48 North Bar Without and behind 22 North Bar Within. At No. 48 the redundant openings were simply infilled, but at No. 22 the builder took advantage of the clause stipulating that adjacent windows with divisions of less than 12 ins. between them counted as one window. Three evenly spaced windows were set in the rear wing, each approximately equal in width to that of the brick pier between them; the end frame was taken out and inserted in place of the brickwork between the remaining two and the hole filled in; thus three windows were henceforth taxed as one. New three-light windows, again to achieve a tax saving, were put into 72–74 Lairgate, 11 Butcher Row and 7 Hengate. The later 17th-century and earlier Georgian windows had leaded lights inset in a plain mullion and transom frame, but by the 1730s the sliding sash became popular, at least for frontages, though thereafter sash windows became commonplace except where economy was paramount; then the 'Yorkshire' sliding sash was used as at 4 Ladygate or in the later Georgian terraces in Minster Moorgate.

From the 1750s there was a change in proportion from the horizontal to the vertical, from the two-storied to the three-storied, from the rural to the distinctly urban house. The change had been anticipated by Colen Campbell's Hotham House, Eastgate, of *c.* 1713–21, and Walkergate House, Norwood House and the Cross Keys Hotel in Lairgate may be seen as representatives of the newer mode. In minor detail, the earlier doorcases were often simply lengthened window openings, as at 36 North Bar Within or 4 Ladygate, but many similar doorways were brought up to date by the addition of enrichment, as at 54 Keldgate or 3–5 Ladygate. From the 1760s the better doorcases had pediments and a little carving, as at 6–8 Newbegin, 55–56 North Bar Within or 39 North Bar Without. Columns were sparingly used, and an early example of *c.* 1765 is at 58 North Bar Without, splendidly enriched with carving, but by the 1790s, as in Hull, tall columned doorcases became more numerous. Good examples can be seen at 40 North Bar Within and at 72–74 Lairgate, all by the firm of William Middleton.

By the 1780s carved ornament was being supplanted by 'composition' ornament, of a synthetic material pressed into moulds. Externally it was used at 33–37 North Bar Without and internally on chimney-pieces at 10 Hengate and 72 Lairgate. The glazing bars on windows also changed from the thick oak bars characteristic of the 1730s or 1740s to the much thinner ones typical of late Georgian and 19th-century windows. Multi-paned sash lights remained common until the later 19th century, though by that time they were used only at the backs of houses. Comparable changes can be detected internally, for wood-panelled walls still lingered in fashion until *c.* 1770, but thereafter wallpaper came into general use and by the late 1830s even cottages had one room papered, though the walls in the remainder were colour-washed.[40] Again, as in Hull, the classical style was maintained with only minor changes of emphasis and detail until, in the latter half of the 19th century, the vernacular was steadily replaced by a style owing more to outside practice. Paradoxically in just those years a vigorous group of carvers and decorators was active whose work was in marked contrast to that shown in the mass-produced decorative materials imported into the area. The firm of James Edward Elwell was of outstanding importance, but its technical skills were applied to the reproduction of any of the historical styles and new work was sometimes cleverly intermixed with fragments of genuine antiquity.

Notes

1 Buildings dating from the 16th century or earlier are indicated on Map 1.

2 The Account Book is deposited at Crust, Todd and Mills, solicitors, Beverley.

3 The large collection of vouchers showing the craftsmen at work at Burton Constable in the mid and late 18th century are deposited at HCRO DDCC/140.

4 A good set is found at Nos. 174–212 Norwood.

5 Poulson, Appendix, 27–48, gives a detailed account defining each property, but see p. 56, n.7.

6 See Hall and Hall, 68–9 for transcript of the full rebuilding lease for Newbegin Bar House, 1744/5.

7 HCRO DDBC 16/132 gives the terms of Samuel Smith's rebuilding lease; he was to take down six tenements and build as many tenements as would fill the space – possibly 49–67 Minster Moorgate.

8 The book is deposited in the offices of Allenby and Wick, North Bar Within.

9 HCRO PE 1 St. Mary's Church. For further details of church properties see de Boer, 51–55 and map 15.

10 HCRO QSF; in Midsummer 1807 Coade and Sealy charged £129 6s. for 'ornaments' and in 1809 charged £21 for the replacement of the statue of Justice, which had broken in transit.

11 Leland, ed. Smith, I, 46–7.

12 These houses were demolished in 1754 and 1759 respectively.

13 Oliver, 267 notes the system of construction. See also Oliver, 294, which refers to the broad, thin bricks of the 'ancient Guildhall'.

14 See for example HCRO DDBC 16/37. However a reference to Beverley tilers *c.* 1385 calls them 'adustores laterum quibus domus plures in Beverlaco et alibi teguntur' (Bond, III, 179).

15 HCRO DDBC 16/64 describes the use of 'Holland tyles' for Timothy Hobson's house, later the Bluecoats School and now 38 Highgate.

16 HCRO PR 177 describes Ralph Featherstone's lease. He was to restore the messuage 'very much out of repair' and rebuild the 'ruinous' stable.

17 Moulded brick cornices occur at 9, 11, 17, (former) 19 Toll Gavel; 15, 33, 35, 37 Highgate; 8–11 St. John Street; 93, 104 Minster Moorgate; 76, Cross Keys and former Manse, Lairgate; 19 and 35 North Bar Within; 5, 5a, 7 Hengate; 90 and 92 Walkergate. Modillion brick cornices are at 38 Highgate; 6, 7, 49–67 Minster Moorgate; 91 Lairgate; 19 North Bar Within; and 12 Hengate. There is a corner brick cornice at 37 Ladygate. Similar examples can be seen at Barton-upon-Humber and at Brigg.

18 Summerson, 43.

19 The Wrightson houses include 90–92 Walkergate, 35 North Bar Within. Middleton's 6–8 Butcher Row and 72–74 Lairgate have fine wooden cornices. Rushworth built 55–59 Toll Gavel, which have a stone string-course.

20 HCRO Registry of Deeds EX 107/120, EX 108/121 describe the site and the 'house which Edward Page is now erecting'.

21 MacMahon 1958, 4. Estimates and subsequent reports occur from 15 Feb. 1762.

22 ibid., 3, 13 Sept. 1711: Mr. Shelton (of Wakefield) showed his drawings of the cross and Mr. Edward Robinson was to buy the wood.

23 ibid., 2 April 1753: plans by Samuel Smith.

24 ibid., 57, 3 March 1777: plans by William Middleton.

25 ibid., 35, 3 Feb. 1755: Mr. Hoggard was to take down the houses and build as many new houses as would take up the foundation space of the old, and re-use old tiles where possible.

26 HCRO DDBC 20/7 includes several plans by Edward Page for the new development, including the one carried out.

27 Edward Page and his son Gregory bought Friar's Close and Trinity Closes (HCRO Registry of Deeds FP 388) in 1849 after the opening of the railways and laid out building plots on Railway Street, Trinity Lane and Wilbert Grove for speculative development (e.g.

HCRO Registry of Deeds GU 90/113).

28 HCRO Registry of Deeds A 105 describes the three cottages and a messuage on the site of the present house.

29 There are frequent references to salvaging of materials in the Corporation Minute Books, e.g. 2 April 1753. Much visual evidence of re-used timbers remains in roofs today. At 7 Hengate an alteration of the 1760s re-used curtain pulley laths and richly carved and gilt mouldings, probably from the newly demolished Hotham House, Eastgate, with which the then owner of No. 7, Dr. J. Johnston, was involved, together with Thomas Wrightson the builder. For further 'finds' from Hotham House see Hall and Hall, 53–4.

30 HCRO DDBC 16/67, 1714 is an indenture concerning land leased to Sir Charles Hotham in Highgate and Eastgate 'intended for improvement by walling or erecting buildings . . . the present building is ruinous', a plot which still remains gardens.

31 HCRO Registry of Deeds CX 599/775 concerns the sale of the site of five cottages bought by John Courtenay *c.* 1794 but 'now a garden'. The *clair-voie* survives on the N. but its S. counterpart, which gave a view of this garden, was presumably removed when that part was sold in the mid-19th century.

32 Oliver, 288 n. Henry Ellison leased four tenements which he was allowed to demolish to enlarge the grounds of his house, St. Mary's Manor, which he was to rebuild. HCRO Registry of Deeds EC 166/182 and CX 76/83 define the various sites.

33 MacMahon 1958, 2, 20 Oct. 1709; Henry Spendlove is given permission to raise the pavement along his 'new built house'.

34 ibid., 48, 4 April 1768; Charles Tennyson, grocer, has to pay 6*d* per annum for his new bow window.

35 Poulson, 447 describes the Assembly Rooms in North Bar Within, to be replaced in 1761/2 by the Norwood Rooms. See also HCRO DDBC 21/95 for building accounts for the latter.

36 HCRO BW529 describes the plot bought in 1754, including the two messuages which were a 'playhouse'.

37 Poulson, 447; HCRO Registry of Deeds CB 66/100.

38 Hall and Hall, 87.

39 HCRO PE 1 St. Mary's churchwarden accounts, indicate much building activity in 1714.

40 E.g. observations during the demolition of School Lane and Spencer Street.

PLATE 12.   Nos. 35 and 37 Ladygate prior to demolition in April 1980.

ARCHAEOLOGY AND DEVELOPMENT IN BEVERLEY

In 1965, when the Council for British Archaeology listed Beverley as one of the 51 British towns 'so splendid and so precious that the ultimate responsiblity for them should be a *national* concern',[1] the town was facing its first serious threat from modern large-scale developments. Major road improvement schemes and proposals to redevelop large sections of the centre provoked widespread concern at both local and national level, and as a result of increasing opposition some of the more drastic proposals were eventually dropped. Those that have been approved are shown in Fig. 12.[2] In recognition of the need to protect the character of the town from unsympathetic modern redevelopment the central area was designated a Conservation Area in 1969, and between 1968 and 1975 the Department of the Environment's List of Buildings of Special Architectural or Historical Interest was extensively revised.

Conservation Area policy in Beverley has been mostly concerned with the historic street pattern and with the large numbers of listed buildings in the town centre. The archaeology of the town below-ground has so far received little attention from either central or local government. In 1972 the report *The Erosion of History* drew attention to the absence of a local museum and to the general lack of provision for archaeology in Beverley, which it included as one of 25 small towns in England urgently in need of archaeological investigation.[3] Some rescue excavation was undertaken in the 1960s and 1970s at the Dominican Friary and in Minster Moorgate, but lack of resources severely restricted the scale of this work and no considered policy for archaeological research in the town was devised until trial excavations were caried out at Highgate in 1977. In the following year a start was made on this present report. The Highgate excavations provided further proof of the town's high archaeological potential and raised a number of important questions about the origins and development of the urban topography. Lack of funds unfortunately prevented further investigation of development sites in the central area and only as recently as the summer of 1979, with the start of the excavation at Lurk Lane by the Humberside Archaeological Unit, was a firm archaeological presence established in the town.

Archaeology, however, does not consist only of excavation, nor does it stop at ground level. The archaeological evidence for Beverley's history comprises all the physical remains of man's past activities on the site of the town, from its first occupation to the present day. The surviving street pattern, property boundaries and standing buildings constitute the uppermost levels of the archaeological stratigraphy, and all are relevant to the study of the town's past. Documentary evidence, too, plays a vital role in the task of reconstructing the history of the earlier communities of Beverley, but for the wide range of human activity omitted from the written accounts and for the early periods without documentation archaeology is our only source of information. The evidence of archaeology and topography, of architecture and of documents, is therefore complementary; each gains much from the existence of the others, and the unrecorded destruction of one form of evidence not only removes part of a town's archive but also diminishes the value of those which are preserved. Archaeology is thus an important way, often the only way, of learning about Beverley's past and of understanding the character and detailed form of the town as it exists today. As was pointed out in a study of Oxfordshire towns, 'this study is more than a purely academic pursuit', for without an appreciation of the 'factors which have shaped a town's present character, measures taken to conserve that character will not be wholly effective or, worse, features basic to its unique identity may be unwittingly destroyed'.[4]

The conservation of buried archaeological evidence in towns presents serious problems, for not only is there the pressure of redevelopment and the high value of urban properties with which to contend, but the sites themselves are often difficult to define or evaluate; their full archaeological potential may only become apparent when an excavation is undertaken in advance of development or by observations made while development is in progress and thus cannot be delayed. Only two archaeological sites in the town, Hall Garth and part of the Dominican Friary, enjoy statutory protection as Scheduled Ancient Monuments, but this protection did not prevent the removal in 1962 of the precinct wall and gateway in Eastgate nor the laying in 1980 of a major pipeline along the W. side of Hall Garth, although it did ensure that some provision was made at the latter site for archaeological investigation of the contractor's trenches.[5]

Because of the difficulties of scheduling urban properties, other sites within Beverley are unlikely to be given the same protection, apart perhaps from sections of the town ditch surviving as earthworks. It is therefore crucial that a concerted effort should be made at local government level to safeguard the sites described in this survey which are known or suspected to have a high archaeological potential, and that adequate provision is made for their investigation in advance of any redevelopment. This might be best achieved by the use of planning constraints and by conditions attached to planning consents.

The fact that Beverley is occupied by a living community means that investigation of its archaeology can only be tackled piecemeal as and when the opportunity arises, and the selection of sites must be related as much to the process of redevelopment as to the needs of research. However, urban excavation is a relatively slow and expensive method of enquiry compared with other forms of historical research, and resources of time, money and manpower are inadequate to excavate each site prior to redevelopment, even if this were academically desirable. An effective archaeological programme must therefore weigh up the potential of each site against research priorities and ensure that certain requirements are fulfilled before selection for excavation.

First, the site should be one known to be likely to contribute to archaeological knowledge of the town; it should be relatively free from modern disturbance. Unless an excavation is directed to answer specific and defined questions or to the examination of linear features such as a street or town ditch, a large site will generally yield more valuable results than a small one. In view of the limited resources available for excavation, priority should be given to sites which are likely to yield information about all periods of occupation rather than one or two, resulting in partial or incomplete sequences. Similarly, excavation should not be confined to exceptional or atypical sites but should also include 'normal' sites providing evidence of typical houses or streets which can then serve as a basis for comparison.

Too few excavations have been carried out in Beverley to enable archaeological deposits to be assessed accurately, but on present evidence a depth of about 2–4m. of stratified deposits is to be expected within the medieval town. This contrasts with a total stratigraphy of 2m. or less in the smaller historic towns of Humberside. Moreover, at Beverley the lower layers in many parts are waterlogged and thus favour the preservation of organic material such as plant remains, wood and leather. Returns from excavation in the town are therefore likely to be exceptional.

The type of development proposed for a site must also be taken into account, for some are more destructive than others. A deep road cutting or basement, for instance, can totally remove archaeological layers, and strip foundations or piling will fragment them, leaving some areas intact. The method of construction also has a bearing on the scale of archaeological operations, and rescue work on proposed building sites is sometimes severely restricted or even prohibited on the grounds of the extra costs that would be incurred as a result of the disturbance caused by archaeological excavations. Demands for reinstatement of a site to a high specification prior to development can constitute an enormous drain on the resources available for the actual work of excavation and can occasionally be so great as to preclude useful work. These problems become particularly acute when dealing with the deepest archaeological deposits, in many respects the most crucial layers, for, as recent excavations in the town have shown, it is precisely these levels that require work over a large area in order to increase the chances of interpreting the often very fragmentary archaeological features. The restrictions placed upon the depth and extent of excavations, sometimes unrealistic, could be reduced if there were better understanding between archaeologist and developer. It is, for instance, often overlooked that archaeologists can provide developers with detailed information on the nature of a site. Many of the problems of building on excavated sites could be resolved if the archaeological prospects and the need for investigation prior to development were taken into account in the granting of planning permission. Indeed, to the extent that redevelopment involves the destruction of part of a town's 'archive', the developer should be persuaded, if possible, to contribute towards the cost of rescue work by partly financing excavation or architectural survey, or to assist archaeology by certain adjustments of building design.

Finally, there must be adequate time in which to excavate. Experience at Hull and other historic towns has shown that, in order to be fully effective, large-scale 'area' excavations require from six to eighteen months. (The Lurk Lane excavations were scheduled to finish in March 1981, nearly twenty months after work began in earnest.) As yet no legal provisions ensure sufficient time for excavation of sites in Beverley prior to redevelopment, and arrangements for access to sites and time for investigation depend at present on the co-operation of individual developers. Negotiation for adequate excavation time is sometimes difficult; in fact rebuilding on smaller sites may occur so fast that there is barely time for negotiation. However, if archaeological factors are taken into account at an early stage in the planning process, the excavation can usually be integrated into the redevelopment programme without causing any delay to contractors.

Wherever excavation is not possible, construction work should be observed by a trained archaeologist. Observation carried out consistently over a number of years can yield

Fig. 12.   Beverley Town Centre: proposed development. A: Hengate – Sow Hill Road, partially completed. B: Sow Hill Road – Dog and Duck Lane, largely completed. C: Dyer Lane – Walkergate, development expected 1982–3. D: Keldgate – Minster Moorgate, development expected 1981–2. E: Lurk Lane – St. Andrew's Street (site of recent archaeological excavations), development to begin mid 1981. F: Manor Road, building postponed. G: Champney Road, building in progress. Walkergate Relief Road completed. Chantry Lane Relief Road, under review. Beverley High Level Scheme, under construction for completion late 1981.

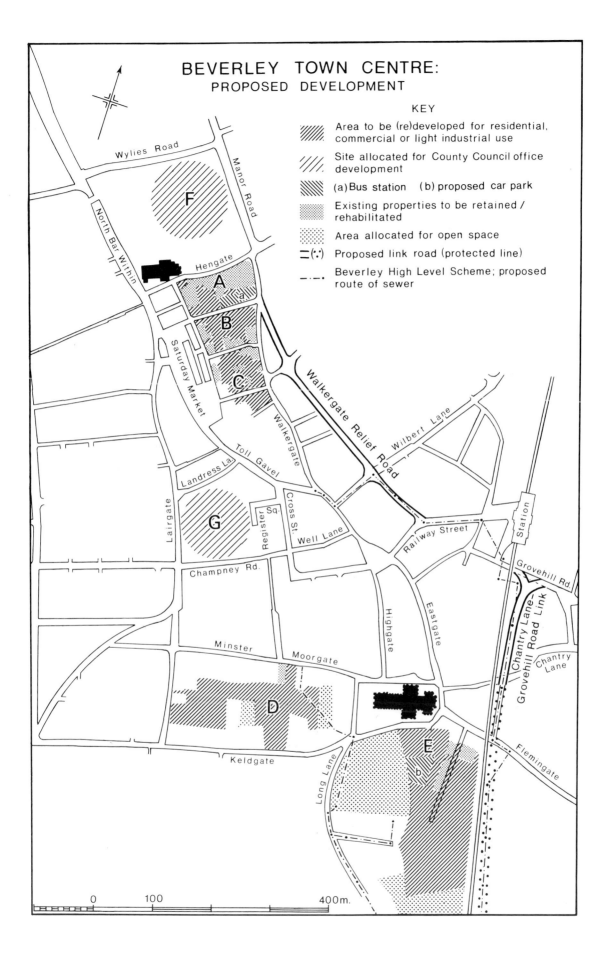

BEVERLEY TOWN CENTRE:
PROPOSED DEVELOPMENT

KEY

Area to be (re)developed for residential, commercial or light industrial use

Site allocated for County Council office development

(a) Bus station   (b) proposed car park

Existing properties to be retained / rehabilitated

Area allocated for open space

Proposed link road (protected line)

Beverley High Level Scheme; proposed route of sewer

Wylies Road

Manor Road

North Bar Within

Hengate

F

A

a

B

C

Saturday Market

Walkergate

Walkergate Relief Road

Wilbert Lane

Toll Gavel

Landress La.

Lairgate

Register Sq.

Cross St.

Well Lane

G

Railway Street

Station

Champney Rd.

Grovehill Rd.

Highgate

Eastgate

Chantry Lane

Grovehill Road Link

Chantry Lane

Minster

Moorgate

D

Keldgate

Long Lane

E

b

Flemingate

0   100   400m.

valuable results with a minimum of expenditure and without inconveniencing the developer. At Beverley, where there is so little information on buried deposits, observation can provide details of their depth and complexity and help to build up a clearer picture of the nature and date of occupation in various parts of the town. Again, there must be close liaison between archaeologists, planners and developers so that appropriate arrangements can be made well in advance.

The retrieval of evidence from threatened standing buildings poses similar problems. Most of the town's buildings dating from before the early 19th century lie within the Conservation Area and have been listed by the Department of the Environment as of special architectural or historical interest. On the Statutory List the Minster and St. Mary's Church are Grade A, seven buildings (the Market Cross, the Guildhall, the North Bar, 65–67 North Bar Within, Lairgate Hall and Norwood House) are Grade I, and 399 buildings are of Grade II.[6] Three important buildings which had been omitted, 11 and 35–37 Ladygate (Plate 12), were added to the List in 1980, but there are still others which deserve a higher degree of protection, notably 131–133 Keldgate (Plate 13), 13–15 Flemingate (Plate 9), 36–40 Beckside and 11a Wednesday Market.

As the demolition of 35–37 Ladygate soon after listing shows only too well, the statutory protection of a building neither guarantees its preservation nor ensures that a full record is made of it before destruction.[7] If the owner gains permission to demolish a listed building he is legally responsible for notifying the Royal Commission on Historical Monuments and affording access, so that the Commission has the opportunity to record the building, but in practice the load of work is such that usually no more than a photographic record is made. If a building to be demolished is unlisted there is no provision at all for recording it. Some such buildings may be of early date but so altered that their real character is not apparent, and important features concealed by later work may only become visible during demolition. Because of this possibility all buildings threatened with demolition should be examined both before work begins and while it is in progress, and a record, including measured drawings and photographs, be made. Provision should also be made for the salvage and storage of significant architectural detail and for its sympathetic re-use. This would have to be funded by the local authority, since the Department of the Environment's funds are for rescue excavation only and the Royal Commission does not have finance to spare for such purposes.

The situation for archaeology in Beverley is now critical. Increased mobility and the expansion of service industries have given the town a new regional significance which is putting increased pressure on its historic fabric. Development is already under way in some areas and plans are in preparation for further substantial redevelopment in the historic town centre. These schemes will involve destruction of archaeological levels more extensive and thorough than ever before in the town's history. At the same time they provide unique opportunities for archaeological investigation and recording which, if not exploited now, will be lost for ever. However, it is only by a substantial increase in the funding of archaeology by both local and national government that the threats posed by redevelopment in Beverley can be met. If action is not taken now much of the history of this remarkable town will pass irretrievably beyond our reach.

PLATE 13.   Nos. 131 and 133 Keldgate, November 1979.

Notes

1 CBA 1965, 1, 6.
2 For an archaeological assessment of these and other schemes see 'Development in Beverley: the archaeological implications', duplicated typescript prepared 1980 for the Humberside Joint Archaeological Committee.
3 Heighway 1972, 95, 126.
4 Rodwell 1975, 11.
5 The other scheduled ancient monuments in Beverley parish are the enclosure and groups of barrows on the Westwood near the Black Mill, the Guildhall, Lairgate Hall and the Saturday Market Cross (Department of the Environment, *List of Ancient Monuments in England as at 31 December, 1977, Vol. I, Northern England* (1977), 26–31).
6 Information provided by Beverley Borough Council from the lists prepared originally by the Ministry of Housing and Local Government and subsequently by the Department of the Environment. For a summary, see the current edition of the extract, *Listed Buildings,* published by the Council.
7 For outspoken comments on their demolition and on other aspects of conservation in Beverley, see SAVE Britain's Heritage, *Newsletter,* March 1981.

APPENDIX

STREET AND PLACE NAMES OF BEVERLEY

The names, which cover the period from the 12th century to the 16th century, are arranged alphabetically. For most only the earliest record and major variations in spelling are given, since a full list of documentary references is beyond the scope of this survey. Later references and names of places on the outskirts not included here will be found in Smith, 192–203; a revised list of the more frequently documented street names is included as an appendix in de Boer. Streets paved or repaired between 1344 and 1502/3 are marked with an asterisk; this includes work on bridges, gutters and sewers. Names in italics have not been positively identified. For an explanation of the abbreviations, see p. 84.

Aldegate 1266; Leach 1903, 292.
    Aldgate 1449/50; KA.
in Beckside area, perhaps present Figham Road.

Alde Newebigging 1340; Martin, 174.
    Aldenewebygyng 1445; KA.
    Old Newbegin 1585; Poulson, Appendix, 28, 33.
perhaps present Morton Lane.

Almot Lane 1445/6; Leach 1898, 97.

alto vico *c.* 1135; Smith, 195.
    alta via 1249–69; Bond ii, 108. 1498; Raine 1868, 133.
the street from North Bar to Fishmarket, now successively North Bar Within, Saturday Market, Toll Gavel and Butcher Row.

Aungerlaneduerant 1449/50; KA.
    Augry lane 1519/20; KA.
a lane skirting the N. side of St. Mary's churchyard.

baker's row (rengea Pistorum) 1329; *CPR 1327–30*, 407.
    Bread Row 1445/6; Leach 1898, 101.
    Brederawe 1502/3; KA.

Bakhouselane 1439; HMC, 123.

*Barleyhome 1344; KA; 1585. Poulson, App. 37.
now Beckside.

le Bekbank 1371; Smith, 197–8.
    Bekhead, Beksyde 1417; Leach 1903, 313.
present Beckside (not including the former Barleyholme).

Belmanlane 1460; KA.

Byscopdinge 1282; Smith, 197.
    Bishopdyngs 1284; HMC, 19.
    *le Dynges 1386; KA.
present Butterdings in Saturday Market.

Blakefreer Lane 1444; Smith, 195.
    Frerelane 1445; KA.
present Friars Lane on the S. side of the Dominican Friary; a 'street in front of the friars preachers' is mentioned in 1318; HMC, 21.

Bolexlane 1329; *CPR 1327–30*, 408.

Boubriggelane 1329; *CPR 1327–30*, 408.
    Bowbriglane 1405; KA.
became Dyer Lane in the 18th cent.

Bradwellane 1445; KA.
on the E. side of the town? – a timber bar was made at its end in 1445 (p. 39).

Briddalmyddyng 1433/4; KA.
    Birdallane 1460; KA.
    Burdall Middyng Lane 1502/3; KA.
    Birdall Widow 1585; Poulson, App. 35.
    Burdat Midding Lane 1681; Leach 1900, 167, 169.
    Burdet Lane 1747; Burrow's map.
present Dog and Duck Lane between Saturday Market and Walkergate.

Buge Row 1500; Smith, 196.

Bulryng 1449; HMC, 133.
the Bullring, formerly on the W. side of Saturday Market.

butcher's market 1329; *CPR 1327–30*, 406, 407.
    *Bocherow 1445; KA.
    rangea carnificium 1445, 1456; HMC, 131, 138.
    Boucher Raw 1460; Raine 1855, 239.
    Street called Fleshe Market 1585; Poulson, App. 29.
in the Cornmarket (later Saturday Market) and/or between the market place and Hengate. There was also a butchers' market in Barley Holme in the 14th cent. (p. 33).

Castell lign 1450/51; KA.
in one of the market places.

Cattfosse Lane 1556; KA.
 Catface Lane 1585; Poulson, App. 43.
present Grayburn Lane between Lairgate and the Leases.

Chapel lane 1434; HMC, 22.
outside Keldgate Bar, perhaps the lane near St. Thomas's Chapel (see p. 48).

Cokewoldgate 1332; BBR Schedule III/12/1.
 Cokwald Strete 1434; HMC, 22.
outside Keldgate Bar, perhaps the present Cartwright Lane leading to the Westwood.

Colmankeld 1502/3; KA.
perhaps the later Coponkeld between Flemingate and Hellgarth.

cornmarket 1329; *CPR 1327–30*, 408.
 Cornemarket 1386; KA.
 Cornmarket 1585; Poulson, App. 32.
now Saturday Market.

Couperlane 1391; Hebditch, 19.
 Couper Lane 1439; HMC, 123.
opposite St. Mary's church, perhaps the present Waltham Lane, previously Kirk Lane.

Coyner Lane 1545; HMC, 179.

*le Crossbrug 1324; BBR Schedule III/2.
 Crosebrig 1344; KA.
the Cross Bridge over the Walkerbeck at the Toll Gavel – Walkergate junction.

le Crossegarth 1320; BBR Schedule III/13.
 Crossegarthes 1376; Clay, 30.
present Cross Street – Register Square area.

Croslane 1502/3; KA.

Dedelane 1327; Smith, 197.
 Deadlane 1585; Poulson, App. 28.
a lane along the E. side of St. Mary's churchyard.

Dings, see Byscopdinge.

Eastgate 1239; Witty, *BG*, 28 Dec. 1929 (from Registers of Archbishop Walter Gray).
 Estgate *c.* 1265; Leach 1903, 293.
present Eastgate.

Ferourlane 1381; B.I.Prob.Reg. I,f.38v.
 Ferrourlane 1440; Hebditch, 24.
on the E. side of Eastgate/Fishmarket.

Fishmarket 1239; Witty, *BG*, 28 Dec. 1929 (from Registers of Abp. W. Gray).
 Fischmarket 1450/51; KA.
became Wednesday Market.

*Fismarketgat 1307; Leach 1897, 206.
 Fishmarketgate 1344; KA.
perhaps the N. approach to Fishmarket.

Fishmarketmoorgate 1320; BBR Schedule III/13.1.
 Fishmarketmoorgate 1501; BBR Sch. III/13.21–2.
present Well Lane.

*Flammengaria 12th cent.; Smith, 195.
 Flemyngate 1221–35; Bond I, 427.
 vicum Flandrensium 1318; Smith, 195.
present Flemingate.

Flyntonlane 1449/50; KA.

Foregate 1202; Brown, W. 1894, 43.

Galdegate 1202; ibid.

Gilegate 1202; ibid.
from St. Giles' Hospital?

Godecheplane 1329; *CPR 1327–30*, 406.
 Goodcheplane 1449/50; KA.
 Goodchepelane 1498; Raine 1869, 133.
off the *alta via*.

Godelane 1329; *CPR 1327–30*, 409.

Graslane 1329; *CPR 1327–30*, 406.

Grenelane 1502/3; KA.

Greystock layn 1556; KA.

Hayrarlane 1402; Smith, 197.
 Hayrerlane 1440; Hebditch, 24.
 Oswaldgate alias Hairelane 1473; B.I.Prob.Reg. IV, f.199v.
now Wilbert Lane; see Oswaldgate.

Hellegarth 1430; HMC, 22.
 lanes in le Hell garthes 1556; KA.
Hellgarth Lane, from Friars Lane to Potter Hill, now largely obliterated by industrial development.

Hengate 1327; Smith, 195.
 Hegate 1417; Leach 1903, 317.
present Hengate.

Heraldlane 1405; KA.

*High Bridge 1409; HMC, 158.
 magni pontis 1417; Leach 1903, 314.
the bridge which formerly crossed the Beck downstream from Low or Parson's Bridge.

Hyegate *c.* 1539; PRO, sc/Henry VIII/4571 m.8.
Highgate 1578; Smith, 195; Leach 1903, 359–60.
the present Highgate, but see p. 20.

Holmekirklane 1400; B.I.Prob.Reg. III, f.59v.
    Holmekyrklane 1417; Leach 1903, 315.
    Holme Church Lane; Poulson, App. 42.
present Holme Church Lane.

le Horsegrene 1329; *CPR 1327–30,* 408.

Humbergate 1332; BBR Schedule III/12/1.
perhaps the later Humber Street, now Queensgate; see
Burrow's map (Fig. 5).

*★Keldgate pre-1279; Hebditch 11.
present Keldgate, but see *Suthbarregate.*

Kyrkleyn 1520; HMC, 173.
    Kirk lane otherwise Waltam Lane 1585; Poulson, App.
    28.
present Waltham Lane on the W. side of North Bar Within.
See Couperlane and *Waltheuelane.*

Kitchen Lane 16th cent.; Witty, *BG,* 28 June 1930.
present Kitchen Lane S. of Keldgate.

Kutstulpyt 1379; Smith, 196.
    Constabularia Kutstulnpyt usque Crosby 1381; *YAJ*
    20 (1909). 323.
    ★Cukstolepit 1392; Smith, 196–7.
    a lane called Cuckstoolpit 1585; Poulson, App. 35.
see pp. 29–44

*★Ladygate 1439; HMC, 123.
present Ladygate; see p. 19.

*★Lathgate 1270; Bond II, 143.
    Lathgate/Laregate 1585; Poulson, App. 37, 42.
present Lairgate.

Lortegate 1307; Leach 1897, 181.
    Lortlane 1445/6; Leach 1898, 94–5.
    Lark Lane 1585; Poulson, App. 41.
present Lurk Lane. De Boer (p. 33) suggests that Lort Lane
was the early name for Long Lane, but 17th and 18th-cent.
references (e.g. HCRO DDBC 16/16; 16/101; 16/161) iden-
tify Lort or Lurt Lane with Lurk Lane.

Markyt Moorgate 1417; Leach 1903, 316.
probably Fishmarketmoorgate (see above).

Matfreylane 1390: B.I.Prob.Reg. I,f.7.
    Mackfray Lane 1585; Poulson, App. 32.
On the W. side of North Bar Within and N. of Wood
Lane.

Mercere Raw 1416; KA.

Mynstir Bowe 1407; KA.
    Mynsterbow 1494; KA.
in or near the Minster Yard (see p. 14).

*★Mynstermoregate pre-1270; *YASRS* 123 (1957), 15.
present Minster Moorgate.

Moregate c. 1265; Leach 1903, 293.
    Moregate lane 1439; HMC, 194.
presumably either Minster Moorgate or Fishmarketmoorgate.

★Nedderlane 1404; B.I.Prob.Reg. III, f.205.
    Neddirlane 1445; KA.

★Newbriglane 1344; KA.

Neubighyng de Layrthorp 1329; *CPR 1327–30,* 405.
    Neubighing near Lathegate 1329; ibid., 408.
present Newbegin, between Lairgate and the modern St.
Mary's Terrace.

★Niwebigginge 1190, 1191; Smith, 196.
probably not the present Newbegin; see n. 24, p. 36.

North Bar Within
    (ward) Constabularia Infra Barr' Boriales 1381; *YAJ*
    20 (1909), 326.
    (street) Highgate within the North Barr 1585; Poul-
    son, App. 32.
    within North Barre 1585; ibid.
It is not always clear whether references are to the ward
or to the street, which formed the N. section of the *alta
via;* see p. 20.

North Bar Without.
    (ward) Constabularia Extra North Bar 1381; *YAJ* 20
    (1909), 321.
    (street) without North Barre 1585; Poulson, App. 40.
It is not always clear whether references are to the ward
or to the street, which in the 18th cent. was also referred
to as Horsefair; see p. 29.

Nontdritlane 1329; *CPR 1327–30,* 407.
    Noutdritlane 1366; Smith, 197.
    Nowedriclane 1449/50; KA.
    Neatedretelane 1585; Poulson, App. 28
a lane between Saturday Market and Hengate.

Norwode 1308; Leach 1897, 223.
    Norwood 1585; Poulson, App. 42.
present Norwood.

Oswaldgate 1327; Smith, 197.
    Oswaldgate alias Hairelane 1473; B.I.Prob.Reg.IV,
    f.199v.
    Oswaldgate 1556; KA.
    Oswaldgate 1585; Poulson, App. 35.
became Cartwright Lane in the late 17th cent. and now
Wilbert Lane. See also Hayrarlane.

*Parsonbryge 1417; Leach 1903, 313.
    Parson brygg 1494; KA.
the bridge at the head of the Beck, now known as Low Bridge.

Paynlane 1445; KA.

Pighill Lane 1585; Poulson, App. 33.
now Manor Road.

Podynglane 1439; HMC, 123
    Pudding Layn 1556; KA.

Poterscarth lane 1329; *CPR 1327–30*, 405.
perhaps synonymous with or near *Pottergate* or *Potterlane*.

Pottergate 13th cent.: Smith, 197.
    Pottergate 1347; *YAJ* 12 (1892), 110.
    Pottergate 1417; Leach 1903, 320.
between Grovehill and Beckside; see *Potterlane* and pp. 32–33.

*★*Potterlane* 1407; KA.
    potter leyn 1519/20; KA.
near Grovehill; see Pottergate.

Potter Hill 1585; Poulson, App. 42.

Potterstartlane 1409; KA.
off Flemingate.

Queengate 1411; HMC, 19.
    Qweynsgate 1494; KA.
present Queensgate; see *Humbergate*.

Queenstreet 1585; Poulson, App. 43.
near the North Bar, not Queensgate.

Ryngandlan 1417; Leach 1903, 317.
    Rygoldlane 1435; HMC, 21.
between Fishmarketmoorgate (Well Lane) and Minster Moorgate; see n. 46, p. 15.

St. Marygate 1416; KA.
the forerunner of Ladygate?

Saterday Market 1560; Poulson, 315.
    Satterdaie Market 1585; Poulson, App. 41.
present Saturday Market, formerly Cornmarket.

Scorbrugh layn 1556; KA.
a lane on the N. side of the town leading to Scorborough?

Sevyerlane 1433/4; KA.
between Flemingate and Hellgarth.

Seyngelylane 1445; KA.
St. Giles' Lane, presumably near St. Giles' Hospital on the W. side of the town; see also *Gilegate*.

Silverlesse Lane 1585; Poulson, App. 32.
had become Silvester Lane by the mid-18th cent., and now largely obliterated by the bus station.

Skepperlane 1460; KA.
near Lurk Lane.

le Smetheraw 1392; Leach 1900, 36.
    rangea faborum 1439; HMC, 123.
    smith's row 1450/51; KA.

Somyrlane 1423; KA.
opposite St. Mary's church; *St. Mary Lane?*

Soutermarket 1326; *YAJ* 12 (1892), 110.
    cobbler's market 1329; *CPR 1327–30*, 407.
    le Shomarket 1364; HMC, 71, 72.
    vico called Soutermarket 1366; *YAJ* 16 (1896), 88.
    Shomarketlane 1437; Smith, 197.
    Shoemaker Lane 1585; Poulson, App. 33.
a lane on the W. side of Ladygate.

Spurier lane 1566; KA.

*★*Spyneslane* 1433/4; KA.
    Spynys(s)hlane 1502/3; KA.
    Spynes lane 1556; KA.
near Walkergate.

Suthmorgate 1323; Smith, 197.

Suthbarregate c. 1250: Leach 1903, 296.
perhaps Keldgate from its junction with Lairgate to the South or Keldgate Bar.

Tentur Lane 1329; *CPR 1327–30*, 409.
    Tentoure Lane 1557; HMC, 179.
the 1329 lane lay near Walkergate; a Tenter Lane is recorded in Holme Church Lane in the 19th cent., see p. 25.

*★*Tolegavell* 1344; KA.
    Towle/Towel Gavell 1585; Poulson, App.29, 35.
present Toll Gavel.

Tothelane 1329; *CPR 1327–30*, 407.

Trinitelane 1445; KA.
present Trinity Lane.

Turne agayn lane 1557: HMC, 179.

Viberlane 1391; Hebditch, 19.
Vicar Lane 1502/3; KA.
    Wyker/Wiker Lane 1585; Poulson, App. 28.
present Vicar Lane on the W. side of North Bar Within.

common ditch del Walkerbeck 1355; BBR Schedule III/2.
    Walkerbek 1433/4; KA.

the name apparently referred to two streams: the one which ran alongside Walkergate, S. through the Cross Garths and along Long Lane to the Mill Dam Drain; another which ran E., perhaps alongside Hellgarth Lane, to join the Beck at Low Bridge. Both are now culverted. See p. 18.

*Walkergate 1327; Smith, 196.
present Walkergate.

Waltheuelane 1202; Brown, W., 1894, 43.
    Walthene lane 1329: *CPR 1327–30*, 406.
    Walthewlane 1449; KA.
perhaps present Waltham Lane but see Couper Lane.

Wedynsday Market 1446; HMC, 131.
present Wednesday Market.

*Wellane 1556; KA.
present Well Lane, formerly Fishmarketmoorgate.

West Masendue lane 1557; HMC, 179.

alba via (white way) 1417; Leach 1903, 319.
    Whyte Lane 1557; Smith, 197.
a lane off Norwood.

Wodlane 1416; KA.
present Wood Lane.

ABBREVIATIONS

BBR   Beverley Borough Records
BDCS   Beverley and District Civic Society, *The Westwood Study*, 2nd. ed., 1969
BG   *The Beverley Guardian*
BI   *The Beverley Independent*
B.I.Prob.Reg.   Borthwick Institute (York) Probate Registry
CBA   Council for British Archaeology
CPR   *Calendar of Patent Rolls*
DB   Domesday Book
ERA   *East Riding Archaeologist*
ERAST   *East Riding Antiquarian Society Transactions*
HCRO   Humberside County Record Office
HMC   Leach, A. F. (ed.), *Report on the Manuscripts of the Corporation of Beverley*, The Royal Commission on Historical Manuscripts, 1900
KA   Town Keepers' Account Rolls, BBR
Med.Arch.   *Medieval Archaeology*
O.S.   Ordnance Survey
PRO   Public Record Office
RCHM(E)   The Royal Commission on Historical Monuments (England)
Sketches   *Sketches of Beverley and the Holderness Hunt*, Beverley 1882
VCH   *The Victoria County History of Yorkshire*, Vol. 3, 1913
Witty   Witty, J. R., articles in the *Beverley Guardian*
YAJ   *Yorkshire Archaeological Journal*
YASRS   *Yorkshire Archaeological Society, Record Series*

Books and articles listed in the bibliography are indicated in the notes to chapters by the name of the author. If more than one work by the same author is listed, these are distinguished by the year of publication.

BIBLIOGRAPHY

Allen, T., *A New and Complete History of the County of York*, London, 1828.

Allison, K. J., *The East Riding of Yorkshire Landscape*, London, 1976.

Armstrong, P., *Excavations at Lurk Lane, Beverley*, Humberside Archaeological Unit, 1980.

Baker, L. (ed.), *Testamenta Eboracensia* I, Surtees Society Publication 4 (1836).

Barley, M. W. (ed.), *The plans and topography of medieval towns in England and Wales*, CBA Research Report 14, London, 1976.

Bilson, J., 1895 'On the discovery of some Remains of the Chapter-House of Beverley Minster', *Archaeologia*, 54 (1895), 425–32.

Bilson, J., 1896 'The North Bar, Beverley', *ERAST* 4 (1896), 38–49.

Bilson, J., 1917 'Beverley Minster: some stray notes', *YAJ* 24 (1917), 221–235.

Bilson, J., 1920 'St. Mary's Church, Beverley', *YAJ* 25 (1920), 357–436.

Bond, E. A. (ed.), *Chronica Monasterii de Melsa* (3 vols.), Rolls Series 43 (1866–8).

Brooks, F. W., *Domesday Book and the East Riding*, East Riding Local History Society, York, 1966.

Brown, G. P., *A Beverley Chronology*, Beverley Public Library, 1973.

Brown, W. (ed.), 1891 *Guisborough Chartulary* II, Surtees Society Publication 89 (1891).

Brown, W. (ed.), 1894 *Pedes Finium Ebor., Regnante Johanne 1199–1214*, Surtees Society Publication 94 (1894).

Brown, W., 1897 'Documents from the Record Office referring to Beverley', *ERAST* 5 (1897).

Brown, W. (ed.), 1906 *Yorkshire Inquisitions* IV, YASRS 37 (1906).

Bulmer, T., *History, Topography and Directory of East Yorkshire*, Preston, 1892.

Carr, R. H. and MacMahon, K. A., 'The Excavation of the Holme Church of St. Nicholas, Beverley', *YAJ* 34 (1939), 399–410.

Champion, B. A., 'The Gilds of Medieval Beverley' in Riden, P. (ed.), *The Medieval Town in Britain*, Cardiff, 1978, 51–66.

Clay, C. T. (ed.), *Yorkshire Deeds* VII, YASRS 83 (1932).

Cobb, G., *English Cathedrals: the forgotten centuries*, London, 1980.

Colgrave, B. and Mynors, R. A. B. (eds), *Bede, Historia Ecclesiastica*, Oxford, 1969.

Cooper, J. M., *The Last Four Anglo-Saxon Archbishops of York*, Borthwick Papers 38, York, 1970.

Cox, J. C., 'William Stapleton and the Pilgrimage of Grace', *ERAST* 10 (1903), 80–106.

de Boer, J., 'The evolution of the town plan of Beverley', undergraduate dissertation (duplicated typescript), St. John's College, Cambridge, 1979.

Dennett, J. (ed.), *Beverley Borough Records, 1575–1821*, YASRS 84 (1932).

Douglas, D. C. and Greenaway, G. W. (eds.), *English Historical Documents 1042–1189*, London, 1953.

English, B. A. and Neave, V., (eds.), *Tudor Beverley*, Beverley, 1973.

Evans, J., *English Art 1307–1461*, Oxford, 1949.

Fallow, T. M. (ed.), *Memorials of Old Yorkshire*, London, 1909.

Farrer, W. (ed.), *Early Yorkshire Charters* I, YASRS Extra Series I (1914).

Forster, J. R. and Brown, G. P., *Beverley Minster, Historical Notes*, 8th ed., Beverley, 1979.

Gillett, E., *A History of Grimsby*, Oxford, 1970.

Goldthorp, L. M., 'The Franciscans and Dominicans in Yorkshire', *YAJ* 32 (1936), 264–320, 365–428.

Greenwell, W., 1877 *British Barrows*, Oxford, 1877.

Greenwell, W., 1906 'Early Iron Age burials in Yorkshire', *Archaeologia* 60 (1906), 251–324.

Hall, I. and Hall, E., *Historic Beverley*, York, 1973.

Harden, G., *Medieval Boston and its Archaeological Implications*, South Lincolnshire Archaeological Unit, 1978.

Harvey, J. H., *The Medieval Architect*, London, 1972.

Hearne, T. (ed.), 1716 *Aluredi Beverlacensis Annales sive Historia de Gestis Regum Britanniae Libris ix*, Oxford, 1716.

Hearne, T. (ed.), 1774 *De Rebus Britannicis Collectanea* (4 vols.), Oxford 1774.

Hebditch, M. J. (ed.), *Yorkshire Deeds* IX, YASRS 111 (1946).

Heighway, C. (ed.), *The Erosion of History – archaeology and planning in towns*, CBA, London, 1972.

Hewett, C., *English Cathedral Carpentry*, London, 1974.

Hiatt, C., *Beverley Minster – an illustrated account of its history and fabric*, London, 1898.

Hope, E., *Guide to the Church of St. Mary, Beverley*, Gloucester, 1969.

Leach, A. F., 1894 'The inmates of Beverley Minster', *ERAST* 2 (1894), 100–123.

Leach, A. F., 1896 'The Building of Beverley Bar', *ERAST* 4 (1896), 26–37.

Leach, A. F. (ed.), 1897 *Memorials of Beverley Minster: The Chapter Act Book*, I, Surtees Society Publication 98 (1897).

Leach, A. F. (ed.), 1898 'A fifteenth century Fabric Roll of Beverley Minster', *ERAST* 6 (1898), 56–103.

Leach, A. F. (ed.), 1899 *Early Yorkshire Schools* I, YASRS 27, (1899).

Leach, A. F. (ed.), 1899A 'A fifteenth century Fabric Roll of Beverley Minster, cont.', *ERAST* 7 (1899), 50–83.

Leach, A. F. (ed.), 1900 *Beverley Town Documents*, Selden Society Publication 14 (1900).

Leach, A. F. (ed.), 1903 *Memorials of Beverley Minster: The Chapter Act Book* II, Surtees Society Publication 108 (1903).

Leland, J. (Smith, L. T. ed.), *The Itinerary of John Leland in or about the Years 1535–1543*, 5 vols, London 1907.

Lister, J. *The Early Yorkshire Woollen Trade*, YASRS 64 (1923).

MacMahon, K. A., 1954 'Beverley Beck', articles in *BG*, June–July 1954.

MacMahon, K. A. (ed.), 1958 *Beverley Corporation Minute Books 1707–1835*, YASRS 122 (1958).

MacMahon, K. A., 1965 *Beverley: a brief historical survey*, Beverley Borough Council, 1965.

MacMahon, K. A., 1967 *The pictorial history of Beverley Minster*, London, 1967.

MacMahon, K. A., 1973 *Beverley*, Dalesman Publications, Clapham, 1973.

Martin, M. T. (ed.), *The Percy Chartulary*, Surtees Society Publication 117 (1909).

Meaney, A., *A Gazetteer of Early Anglo-Saxon Burial Sites*, London, 1964.

Miller, K. R., 'Development in Beverley: the archaeological implications', Humberside Archaeological Unit, 1980 (duplicated typescript).

Nolloth, H. E., *Beverley Minster and its Town*, 3rd. ed., London, 1952.

Oliver, G., *The History and Antiquities of the Town and Minster of Beverley*, Beverley, 1829.

Palmer, C. F. R., 'The Friar Preachers or Black Friars of Beverley', *YAJ* 7 (1881–2), 32–43.

Pevsner, N., *York and the East Riding*, London, 1972.

Platt, C., *The English Medieval Town*, London 1976.

Poulson, G., *Beverlac; or the antiquities and history of the town of Beverley . . .* , London, 1829.

Raine, J. (ed.), 1855 *Testamenta Eboracensia* II, Surtees Society Publication 30 (1855).

Raine, J. (ed.), 1864 *Testamenta Eboracensia* III, Surtees Society Publication 45 (1864).

Raine, J. (ed.), 1868 *Testamenta Eboracensia* IV, Surtees Society Publication 53 (1868).

Raine, J. (ed.), 1879 *The Historians of the Church of York and its Archbishops* I, Rolls Series 71 (1879).

Raine, J. (ed.), 1884 *Testamenta Eboracensia* V, Surtees Society Publication 79 (1884).

Raine, J. (ed.), 1886 *The Historians of the Church of York and its Archbishops* II, Rolls Series 77 (1886).

Ramm, H. G., *The Parisi*, London, 1978.

Reynolds, S., *An Introduction to the History of English Medieval Towns*, Oxford, 1977.

Rodwell, K., *Historic Towns in Oxfordshire: a survey of the new county*, Oxford, 1975.

Salzman, L. F., *Building in England down to 1540*, Oxford, 1967.

Sheahan, J. J. and Whellan, T., *History and Topography of the City of York and the East Riding of Yorkshire*, II, York, 1856.

Smith, A. H., *The Place-Names of the East Riding of Yorkshire and York*, English Place-name Society 14, Cambridge 1937.

Squire, A., *Aelred of Rievaulx*, London, 1969.

Stead, I. M., 1965 *The La Tène Cultures of East Yorkshire*, York, 1965.

Stead, I. M., 1979 *The Arras Culture*, York, 1979.

Stenton, D. M. (ed.), *The Great Roll of the Pipe for the Fourth Year of King John*, Pipe Roll Society New Series 15 (1937).

Stephenson, W., 'Beverley in Olden Times', *Archaeological Journal* 52 (1895), 271–9.

Stubbs, W. (ed.), *Chronica Magistri Rogeri de Hovedene*, Rolls Series 57 (1869).

Summerson, J., *Georgian London*, London, 1945.

Taylor, H. M. and Taylor, J., *Anglo-Saxon Architecture*, Cambridge, (I, II) 1965 and (III) 1978.

Thompson, A. H., 'Notes on Colleges of Secular Canons in England', *Archaeological Journal* 74 (1917), 139–239.

Turner, H. L., *Town Defences in England and Wales*, London, 1970.

Wilson, D. M. (ed.), *The Archaeology of Anglo-Saxon England*, London, 1976.

Witty, J. R., Articles in *BG*, 1929–30.

NOTES ON THE PLATES

1. *Aerial view of Beverley from the S., the Minster in the foreground.* Below Keldgate, on the S. side of the Minster, a line of trees divides Hall Garth (to the left) from the site of the Lurk Lane excavations (the Bedern ?). The surviving building of the Dominican Friary lies to the left of the footbridge over the railway, almost surrounded by factory buildings. The lines of Eastgate and Highgate meet above the Minster in the triangular Wednesday Market. St. Mary's Church appears near the top centre, standing out against trees in the grounds of St. Mary's Manor. Below it is Saturday Market and immediately to the left North Bar Within and Without continue to the top edge. The former cinema on the site of the Assembly Rooms is prominent to the right of the church at the junction of Manor Road and Norwood. At the top left part of The Hurn appears as open space.

2. *The E. end of the Minster from Flemingate, from a late 19th-century postcard.* On the extreme left is the W. end of a group of single-storied buildings; beyond, at the corner of Flemingate and Minster Yard South, is a substantial jettied timber-framed building. A similar view in Johnson's *Outline views of Beverley Minster* (*c.* 1850) and an undated watercolour in Beverley Library show the same building with great timber arched braces in its E. gable. Here the gable is plastered, but some elements of the frame show in the discolouration of the stucco covering. This group was demolished *c.* 1912 to make way for the Constitutional Hall. The Sun Inn, a jettied timber-framed house on the opposite side of the street, survives.

3. *North Bar from the N.* The Bar, built in 1409–10, is the most elaborate of the three town gates of which the appearance is known. The entrance is boldly arched within a hoodmould, like that of Newbegin Bar, and on the N. side is framed by wide buttresses. The upper room is lit by small cusped-arched windows linked by a string course. Above, where there is now another arched light, this 18th-century sketch shows a simple square window. The decorative cornice is surmounted by massive stepped battlements, suggesting Continental influence; the inner face of the Bar has only vestigal buttresses framing the battlements.

    To the E. of the Bar a Gothic building with an arched doorway between two-light traceried windows with three smaller windows above is apparently the medieval St. Mary's Hospital. It was replaced in 1793–4 by the present pair of houses within and without the Bar. The present pavement and pedestrian archway cut across the site of its façade.

4. *Keldgate Bar from the W.* The Bar, demolished in 1808, was two-storied with a segmental-arched opening flanked by buttresses and a plain gable below a steeply pitched roof. A simple string course and gabled niches in the upper part of the buttresses were the sole decoration. The flanking cottages to the S. (right) are similar to those in Plate 13.

5. *Newbegin Bar from the W.* The Bar, rebuilt in 1409–10 and demolished in 1790, adjoined the present Newbegin Bar House of *c.* 1747, to which it was attached at the S.E. corner. Consequently the present main front of the house has no doorcase. The Bar has a boldly arched gateway within a hoodmould, a simple window to the room above the passageway, and was crowned by battlements. It is shown without buttresses, though the length of walling on the N. (left) side suggests the possible intention of building a curtain wall.

6. *The Dominican Friary from the S., November 1979.* The building was photographed while undergoing restoration. The 16th-century gateway in the precinct wall, visible in the foreground, was formerly capped by an elaborate Dutch gable.

7. *North Bar Within, painted by George Barrett c. 1776/7.* This view, presumably commissioned by William Constable (1721–91), for whom Barrett (*c.* 1730–84) also painted views of Burton Constable, is listed in the Constable Inventory of 1791 and is the earliest known view of the town, as distinct from the Minster. None of the houses in the foreground survives: those immediately to the left of St. Mary's Church were demolished in the 1820's to improve the prospect of St. Mary's Manor, of which the Baroque pilastered front appears below the church tower. The house on the left-hand edge was probably that built *c.* 1716 for the surgeon Robert Haslefoot by the Butlers, carpenters, and is shown on the O.S. map of 1854. The group to the right of the church is largely intact, but Kemp's corner on the extreme right was demolished in the 1950's. The W. turrets of St. Mary's were replaced in the restoration by Pugin *c.* 1844, but are preserved at Woodmansey, in part at 7 Hengate and in the Register House Garden, Champney Road.
    St. Mary's Manor and its 4-acre garden were much visited in the early Georgian period, when it was the town house of the Moysers. The pilastered front is the grander version of the theme in the passage of the former George and Dragon (now the Monk's Walk), Highgate. The bold shell hood suggests a date of *c.* 1690 and its double console brackets may be those now on the door of the Push Inn, Saturday Market. Barrett's detail is not, however, wholly trustworthy.

8. *No. 49 North Bar Within, November 1979.* This house, at the corner of Tiger Lane, is probably 15th-century. The front panels are filled with bricks set on edge; the gable-end panels are plastered over above the jetty and brick-filled below. A blocked window with moulded wooden mullions is visible on the ground floor beneath the jetty, of which some brackets survive on the side to Tiger Lane.

9. *No. 15 Flemingate, November 1979.* The E. side was exposed in 1970 after the demolition of adjacent property. The timber framing of this E. wing of a once larger house, now subdivided, is comparable to that shown in Plate 11.

10. *Walkergate, the N. end, looking N., c. 1900.* This view shows the street prior to the demolition of cottages for the building of Walkergate School (1907). The E. side is otherwise still intact. The W. side was largely demolished piecemeal for road widening in the 1960's. The single-storied cottages on the left have two-panelled doors of late 17th or 18th-century character. The houses to the right, beyond the narrow entrance to Silvester Lane, are typical of the later 18th century, but that with the projecting porch is much older. The house with the stone angle quoins, which bore mason's marks on their bedding surfaces, closed the vista along Norwood and was built *c.* 1800 by Appleton Bennison.

11. *Nos. 33–9 Butcher Row, pre-1912.* These houses were on the E. side near the junction with Wednesday Market and were demolished *c.* 1916 to make way for the Marble Arch Cinema. The left-hand house with its string-moulded cornice is typical of the later 17th century in Beverley and Hull. The stucco-fronted house had a narrow (medieval?) plot width and the stucco probably hid a timber frame similar to that of its neighbours to the S.

12. *Nos. 35 and 37 Ladygate prior to demolition in April 1980.* Both had been listed two weeks earlier as Grade II buildings of special architectural or historical interest. No. 35 had a late medieval timber frame and a massive central chimney stack; No. 37 was an early Georgian refronting of an earlier building.

13. *Nos. 131 and 133 Keldgate, November 1979.* Such single-storey cottages were commonplace in Beverley until the last quarter of the 19th century. This 18th-century pair, now threatened with demolition, are the sole survivors. The type, still to be seen in local farmhouses, as in Long Lane, at Tickton, etc., might also be paralleled in Flanders.

Note. In addition to the drawings and photographs used as illustrations, there is a collection in Beverley Art Gallery and Museum and an album of the work of Luke Clennell (1781–1840) in Beverley Local History Library. Clennell made pen and wash drawings of street scenes and individual buildings in Beverley during the 1840's. However, most of these were being re-mounted and were consequently unavailable for use while this report was being prepared.

THE COVER ILLUSTRATIONS

FRONT   North Bar Within, painted by George Barrett *c.* 1776/7. See note on Plate 7.

BACK   A fantastic beast from the reverse of a *sceatta* of King Eadberht of Northumbria (737–58). The coin, here shown five times its actual size, was found on the Lurk Lane site.

INDEX

Page numbers in bold type indicate main entries; numbers in italic indicate illustrations. References to the left and right columns of the text are respectively identified by the letters 'a' and 'b' after the page numbers. The letters 'n' or 'nn' indicate footnotes. Modern versions of street and place-names are used where possible. Names and features shown on the maps or mentioned only in the Appendix have not been indexed.

BEVERLEY: an Archaeological and Architectural Study

The town of Beverley grew up around the monastery 'in the wood of the men of Deira' where John, the saintly bishop of York, was buried in 721. His tomb and the church sheltering it were already a place of pilgrimage by the time of the Norman Conquest and remained a richly endowed shrine and a sanctuary until the 16th century.

This study discusses the splendid Minster church of St. John and its collegiate buildings, the origins and development of the medieval town, a prosperous centre of cloth manufacture, its markets, streets, and suburbs, especially the industrial and commercial area beside the canalised Beck. The remains of the earthwork defences with four brick and stone gateways, of which only one survives, are surveyed in detail for the first time. Descriptions of the medieval public buildings, churches, friaries and hospitals, are followed by a discussion of the houses built during the 17th, 18th and 19th centuries, their construction and details. A final section considers the implications of increased development in the town and the necessity to allow time for archaeological excavation and architectural recording if more is to be discovered of the origins of this unique town.

The many street and place names of medieval Beverley, painstakingly traced from the rich documentary sources, are listed in an appendix. The whole study is illustrated with line drawings and photographs.

Preceding publications in the **Supplementary Series** *of the Royal Commission on Historical Monuments (England):*

1. Liverpool Road Station, Manchester: an historical and architectural survey (Manchester University Press, 1980)
2. Northamptonshire: an archaeological atlas (RCHM, 1980)
3. Early Industrial Housing: The Trinity Area of Frome (HMSO, 1981)

Printed in England for Her Majesty's Stationery Office by Bamber Press Ltd, Greenford, Middlesex
Dd 717070   C40